marijuana flower forcing

SECRETS OF DESIGNER GROWING

by tom flowers

ISBN # 0-9647946-1-6
Third printing 1999

CORRESPONDENCE TO:
Flowers Publishing Company
P.O. Box 5666
Berkeley, CA 94705
fax: 510 595 3779

DISTRIBUTED BY:
(USA & Canada)
Publishers Group West
tel: 800 788 3123
fax: 510 658 1834

(Netherlands)
Sensi Seed b.v.
tel: (010) 477 3033
fax: (010) 477 8893

(United Kingdom)
Avalon
tel: (01) 705 293 673
fax: (01) 705 780 444

(Norway)
Scorpious Imports
tel: (47) 223 740 41
fax: (47) 223 731 36

(Australia)
Agung Trading Company
tel: (06) 280 7266
fax: (06) 280 7367

marijuana flower forcing

SECRETS OF DESIGNER GROWING

tom flowers

Design: Studio Graphik, SF
Photography by Tom Flowers (except where noted)
Photos page 35 and back cover compliments of Grobot International,
    The Netherlands
Illustrations by John F. Davies
Edited by Dana Cannazopolous

Dedicated to
Medical Marijuana Patients

"There comes a time when the operation of the machine becomes so odious, makes you so sick at heart, that you can't take part, you can't even passively take part. And you've got to put your bodies on the gears, and upon the wheels, upon the levers, upon all the apparatus. And you've got to make it stop."

Mario Savio
1943–1996

table of contents

foreword

Marijuana could be called the ultimate sun plant. If given enough light, it is one of the world's fastest growers, surpassing most of Man's other food and herbaceous crops.

But of more interest to the marijuana cultivator is how the plant's flowering cycle is highly regulated by the light and darkness the plant receives. From birth, marijuana is genetically programmed to flower when the length of the night cycle reaches a set point. Once the right darkness cycle is reached and sustained, marijuana will flower. It matters very little whether the plants are young or mature.

It's no secret that many marijuana cultivators are harvesting several crops of flowers a year. They are doing this by regulating the amount of darkness that their plants receive. This is the key to marijuana flower forcing. Not much else but a healthy growing environment is needed. No chemical or hormones are needed to induce marijuana to flower. Only long cycles of uninterrupted darkness.

A well developed sense of how the flowering cycle of marijuana can be regulated gives the grower all kinds of options. A plant's characteristics such as height, branching and maturity date can be adapted more easily to suit the needs of the cultivator; "designer marijuana plants" might be an appropriate term.

Need a two foot plant that will fit in a closet and will grow under fluorescent light? Want an early or late crop in a greenhouse? Think the only way you could get away with growing outdoors is if you could harvest in August? Want to know which light cycle will give you the biggest flowers? Growers across the nation have been pondering just such questions. This book is a report on their experiments. It explores any growing technique that significantly increases the flowering potential of marijuana.

Flower Induction and Beyond

Beyond the direct method of manipulating the flowering cycle of marijuana with light and darkness cycles, many other high-tech growing techniques are being employed to cultivate marijuana. Carbon dioxide enrichment, for example, increases both the rate of growth and size of the flowers. It also increases the number of female plants when seeds are used in cultivation. The "sea of green" technique, where many smaller plants - rather than a few larger plants - are cultivated, has been shown to significantly increase the overall yield under electric lights. Even simple things like the judicious use of the fertilizer phosphorous is known to significantly increase flower size in marijuana compared to phosphorous deficient plants.

Other high-tech growing methods such as using cuttings for propagation rather than seeds does the obvious – it cuts the number of plants that are started in half compared to most seed crops because there are no male plants. The use of cuttings, flower forcing, "sea of green", and CO_2 enrichment leads to a rapid turnover of crops. Many growers harvest 6 or more crops a year. This rapid turnover has had positive secondary effects. It has made it easy for growers interested in breeding plants to easily fix advantageous traits within a seed line.

Other underground botanists are inducing plants to produce seed that will grow crops with either a high percentage of, or all, female plants. Several techniques and treatments are known to have an effect on the number of female plants. It is possible to grow all female crops from seed. This book will tell you what the current research is and what conclusions have been reached thus far.

Some of the information offered comes from work done on plants other than Cannabis and will be mentioned only if it has been tried by marijuana cultivators, or seems to have general application in horticulture. An example meeting both criteria would be the use of the plant hormone ethylene to increase the number of female plants in seed crops. This phenomenon was first noticed in orchid trees that were exposed to the hormone. Several reports from marijuana cultivators show positive results using ethylene treatments on seeds before they are sprouted. Ethylene treatments used at other times, like during the flowering cycle, are more likely to have adverse effects. Since when, as well as how, a substance is applied to a marijuana plant is as important as the substance itself, this book explains how and when to apply flower enhancing substances for best results.

Considering the high-tech way in which marijuana is being grown, very few poisonous substances need be employed in its cultivation. Generally speaking, marijuana cultivators employ both the high-tech, like hydroponics and "sea of green" growing techniques, and many also use organic growing methods and natural insect control. Most of the substances described in this book, like carbon dioxide, are naturally occurring, and used in large amounts by marijuana plants, or are naturally occurring hormones produced by the plant.

Of course, naturally occurring substances like hormones can have very powerful effects. But considering the forces being used to stop the cultivation of marijuana, one has to at least consider all the possibilities. With the authorities squandering billions of dollars trying to run marijuana cultivators out of business, it's no wonder growers seek advantage where they may. The research landscape of the marijuana cultivator more nearly resembles Dodge City than the picket fences of a quaint university town. Still, worthwhile research is being conducted and breakthroughs are being made. Cultivation has moved from the forest to the garage, basement or greenhouse, at great expense to human rights and electricity. But cultivators are adaptable a breed as Cannabis Sativa itself.

I present this material not to turn you all into stoner professors; but because control of the genetic material of the Cannabis plant will become more and more important as the plant moves towards legalization. Forget the cannabinoids, forget the analogs - the government's got the rights locked up tight. Instead of doing the basic research necessary to produce effective cannabinoid based drugs, the government has licensed only one extremely expensive drug, drobinol (Marinol®). It is 4 to 5 times more expensive (measured by the amount of THC contained) than the kindest bud available on the illicit market.

What the big boys don't have control over is the living plants. Right now much of this genetic material, (seeds and cuttings), is held by small outlaw breeders. They have done incredible things with marijuana, considering the conditions they are forced to work under. When you consider that just 20 years ago marijuana could only be grown successfully outdoors in a small area of the United States; and that indoor growing under lights was hardly known, advances in breeding and cultivation techniques have been rapid. With just a few years of research, varieties of potent marijuana have been developed that can mature outdoors throughout the United States and much of Canada. With high intensity discharge lighting pot can be grown virtually anywhere.

The surveillance helicopters and planes that made it necessary for many growers to move indoors under lights, or into greenhouses, have inadvertently spawned new methods of growing marijuana. By using flower forcing techniques and electric lights, growers soon learned that with the right methods, indoor growing has many advantages – such as several harvests each year. Greenhouse growers also have found methods of inducing marijuana to flower out of season and produce several crops a year. For marijuana breeders, multiple crops each year are like manna from heaven. Each harvest means new seed and a new chance at perfection. Much of the breeding of seeds, even for outdoor crops, is now being done indoors under lights.

I include a section on breeding marijuana because flower forcing techniques and multiple harvests have made it possible to make much progress in a short amount of time. Seeds also become very important if you want to stop growing for awhile. Smart growers don't overstay their welcome. With flower forcing and multiple crops any grower can do small scale breeding. So seed up, and move on, and stay one step ahead of "the man".

Still, I doubt that I can impart the "way" some breeders seem to have with Cannabis. A lot of breeding is playing the odds, but the best breeders seem to have an intuitive sense of which plants to pair. The best I could get out of them was that it was like a "vision" thing. Nonetheless, much is possible, even on a small scale without a grand scheme. While savvy horticultural types probably won't be happy until they create the ultimate hybrid, other breeding goals are more easily reached. Some of these include stabilizing seed groups and hybrids, or making crosses with similar kinds of plants. Seeds that will grow high numbers of, or all female plants are also possibilities.

The term "Flower Forcing" may sound a bit harsh. "Flower Induction" has a more gentle ring to it. I use the term "Forcing" because of the difficult existence the Cannabis plant has had for the last fifty years. If the drug war is anything, it's an inquisition where force is used with regularity. The laws against marijuana are easy enough to see as some kind of cruel joke, the wrong move and seizure and jail await you. Funny and absurd, not real. Unless you're caught.

We are spending more on building prisons than on building schools, and many schools resemble prisons anyway. Rational discourse is discouraged as adults live in fear of being arrested by the "Dare Police" after being turned in by their children or by random drug tests at work.

Successful growers are content to stay out of the narcos way. They move around a lot, change identity, don't tell people what they're up to, and generally fade into the woodwork. The people who do best at it are the ones who can adapt to a semi-monastic lifestyle and have stable long-term friends. This is not a job for party animals or the brain dead, as bad moves can be costly.

Most growers interviewed for this work were hardly ready to quit. Instead, they move deeper into the underground. As one cultivator told me, "I would prefer not to grow pot like this, but we are either forced to give up, or forced to use the power of the plant. I use it's power as my guide". The plant species Cannabis Sativa including Marijuana, has proven to be very adaptable, a force to be reckoned with.

1

the force

Inducing plants to flower is a science that has been developed primarily in the 20th century. It is used extensively in legal commercial flower production, pursued in greenhouses around the world. Growers using flower forcing techniques essentially trick their plants into flowering. This is done by simulating the same environmental conditions that spur these plants into flowering in the wild.

With the use of flower forcing techniques these growers cultivate many plants year round. Without some kind of flower forcing techniques many greenhouse flowers, like chrysanthemums, amaryllis or tulips, would only be available during a single season each year. By understanding the life cycle of the plant being grown, these growers are able to make many species of plants flower at will. Harvests are often timed to periods of peak demand.

Not all plants are susceptible to flower forcing, but of the ones that are, certain environmental factors clearly trigger the flowering response. In marijuana, the plant must have a certain number of hours of uninterrupted darkness during each day, or 24 hour period, for the plant to bloom.

Though the darkness cycle is the primary factor used to induce flowering in marijuana, several other growing factors are essential to consider when forcing flowers. These growing factors, though they are not enough by themselves to induce flowering, can either stimulate or repress the flowering response.

Some of these factors include: the nutrient content of the growing medium, the color spectrum of the light used for growing, carbon dioxide in the growing area, and the health and general vigor of the plant.

Cannabis was the subject of the first experiments that conclusively demonstrated that certain plants can be induced to flower out of season. Since the botanist involved has never been properly credited, I will mention a bit of his work here.

In 1910, French botanist Julian Tournois published a paper describing how he induced his greenhouse hemp plants into an early summer flowering. Tournois' discovery laid the foundation for the methods used today throughout the legal commercial flower industry.

Tournois' initial observation was that hemp, when started in his greenhouse during the winter months, flowered at a very juvenile plant stage. Suspecting that it was the short days of winter that had stimulated his plants to flower, he conducted a number of experiments to test his hypothesis.

In some of these experiments he used specially designed light-tight boxes, into which he would wheel his plants on a cart, at certain set times each day. In effect, he was artificially shortening the daylength. With this method he was successful in making his plants flower at his discretion.

But Tournois was only partly right – it was not exactly the short days that induced the flowering. Subsequent research by other scientists verified that it was actually the long nights – the uninterrupted darkness – that induced the hemp to produce flowers. If the darkness cycle is interrupted with only a few minutes of light, even from a relatively weak light source, cannabis can be prevented from flowering. Interrupting the light cycle with periods of darkness has little effect on whether Cannabis flowers.

The terminology, however, was already set, and so today we have a somewhat confusing set of terms to describe plants like Cannabis.

Marijuana is known as a short-day plant. This term describes the mechanism that triggers flowering. Though a "short day" implies that there will be a long night to follow, a more accurate description of marijuana would be that it is a "long night" plant.

Another term, "photoperiod", is used to describe the length of time a plant is exposed to light each day. It is often used in reference to flowering. (Most strains of marijuana will flower in a photoperiod of 12 hours, for example.) This sounds right, but you could have 6 hours of light followed by 6 hours of darkness followed by 6 more of light and then 6 more of dark. Your plants will not flower under these conditions. We will use the term "photoperiod" in this book because it is in general use. When the term photoperiod is used it will mean a certain number of consecutive hours of light, followed by a certain number of hours of uninterrupted darkness, adding up to 24 hours. A 13 hour photoperiod assumes 11 hours of darkness, for example. A 12 hour photoperiod is followed by 12 hours of uninterrupted darkness. None of this will cause any problem so long as it is understood that for marijuana it is the night, the uninterrupted darkness, that triggers the bloom.

Besides laying the foundation for forcing flowers in greenhouses, Tournois' papers set off a search for the mechanism in plants that could read the length of the night, as well as the chemical the plant must produce to induce flowering. Scientists were so sure they would find the substance that they gave it a name, florigen. It was speculated that once this chemical or hormone was found, plants could easily be treated and induced to flower whenever the grower chose.

Florigen, however, proved to be illusive and has never been found, even as many other plant hormones and building blocks of life have become understood. It is still possible that a substance or group of substances will be discovered that will trigger the flowering sequence in certain plants. But even without florigen, Tounois' work pointed the way to many techniques that can be used to induce plants like marijuana to flower.

A plant's method of reading time remains a mystery, although it is known that this activity takes place in the plants' leaves. Plants like marijuana are precise readers of time. In the wild the plant's life depends on this reading of time. Seed must be set before the frost. The plant anticipates the frost by the lengthening of the nights after the summer solstice. In some grow rooms you can almost hear the plants ticking away like fine timepieces.

Marijuana — The Specs

Marijuana is a member of the highly variable, but single, species of plant called Cannabis Sativa. This species includes all the many different drug varieties as well as hemp plants, which are used for fiber and seed. At least two distinct varieties of marijuana are known, Cannabis Sativa and Cannabis Indica. Another variety, Cannabis Ruderalis, has unknown origins, but is believed to be naturalized hemp (Cannabis Sativa) by some, rather than a distinct variety. Some scientists recognize each of these varieties as a distinct species. However, the varieties easily interbreed and produce viable seed, which is indicative of a single species.

All but a few of the varieties of marijuana are highly susceptible to flower forcing. Since most of these non-forcible varieties are hemp, rather than drug plants, marijuana cultivators will seldom see varieties that long nights will not stimulate into flower production. Both male and female marijuana plants will flower if exposed to long nights of continuous darkness.

Most marijuana will flower if given 12 hours of uninterrupted darkness during each 24 hour day cycle. This has become the standard flowering photoperiod for indoor growers.

The precise night cycle needed to induce a particular variety of marijuana to flower is genetically programmed. The latitude of origin of the plant in large part determines the exact lighting and darkness needed. Generally speaking the further north the plant originates the earlier in the year it will begin to flower outdoors. Some Afghani varieties (from latitude 35), for example, will flower in nights as short as 10 hours.

Latitude 35 is the limit of where drug varieties of marijuana are either indigenous or have been cultivated from antiquity. As a species, Cannabis has been cultivated for so long that truly wild strains of what is thought to be indigenous plants have not been found. Except for strains of Cannabis that have escaped cultivation and naturalized, the plant's genome is held by humans.

Tropical varieties of marijuana, like Thai or Columbian, usually require longer darkness cycles to flower than plants indigenous to more temperate regions. Days and nights in equatorial regions vary less than northern locations. Though most of the tropical varieties of marijuana will flower in the standard cycle of 12 hours light and 12 hours of darkness, some will do better in longer darkness cycles. Tropical varieties of marijuana are seldom grown outdoors because they may not complete flowering until December.

Whatever the lighting requirements needed for flowering, plants – like people – are adapted to Circadian rhythms, the 24 hour day and night cycle. Flowering and vegetative cycles that don't add up to 24 hours will confuse the plant and could delay flowering. Some growers, for example, speculated that the 12 hour on, 12 hour off cycle used to flower marijuana under lights could be used in other multiples, 13 hours on, 13 off, or 15 hours on, 15 hours off – essentially any number of hours where the lights are on and off for equal periods.

However, Circadian rhythms rule. Though you might fake out a marijuana plant with the 13 hour cycle, some adverse effects and alterations, such as flower elongation, will be seen. The higher the number of hours in the cycle, the more apparent the alterations will become. Cycles of unequal lengths that are over 24 hours, like 13 hours on, 15 off, will have the same kind of negative effects. In short, marijuana, besides having a system that counts the number of hours of darkness, bases its system on the 24 hour day/night cycle.

Marijuana will grow vegetatively indefinitely if given 16-24 hours of light each day, although each variety has a maximum size. The continuous light cycle (lights on 24 hours a day) used during the vegetative growth stage rapidly stimulates growth. It is somewhat controversial. Growers using 18 hour light cycles often think the 24 hour cycle is unnatural or does not seem to make the plants grow faster. Though it is somewhat unnatural (as is growing under electric lights), marijuana plants – even cuttings – do well in continuous light. In fact, the plant grows proportionately faster than in shorter cycles – 25% faster in continuous light compared to the 18 hour light cycle. Because of the increase in growth, plants grown in continuous light need more water and fertilizer than those in shorter light cycles. Carbon dioxide use also increases (see Chapter 5). If the grower is having difficulty meeting the needs of the plant, shorter light cycles might make sense.

Outdoors, the nightlength after June 21 increases slowly. Each night is 2-5 minutes longer than the last. The nightlengths increase fastest in northern areas. Sometime in late July or early August the days get short enough to trigger the flowering of marijuana. Indoor growers using lights sometimes try to simulate this gradual lengthening of nights. These growers usually decrease the daylength 1/2 hour per week starting at 14 hours (lights on 14 hours, off 10). Daylengths are shortened until the 12 hours on, 12 off, cycle is reached.

Though marijuana can certainly be grown like this there is little evidence that it is beneficial. Flower size, for example, is not increased by using this technique. The technique will also increase the length of the flowering cycle.

Don't Get Critical

Every variety of marijuana has what is known as a "critical nightlength" (Note: horticultural literature calls it "critical daylength".) This is the precise number of hours of darkness the marijuana needs to fully ripen. Outdoors, in natural light, this point is reached late in the flowering stage, at about the 6th week of an 8 week flowering cycle. The marijuana will start to flower in the shorter nights early in flowering cycle, but if that nightlength were sustained a full blooming cycle would not occur. If the night were 11 hours and 30 minutes, for example, on this "critical night", this would be the minimum number of hours of darkness that could be used to fully ripen this plant. This plant's critical nightlength is 11 hours and 30 minutes.

If you wanted to, you could find the critical nightlength and supply the precise amount of light and darkness needed by a particular marijuana strain. But except in a few cases, there is rarely a reason to be so precise. Almost all varieties of marijuana will mature in nights and days of equal length (12 hours). The reason that the "critical nightlength" is not so critical is that marijuana actually flowers faster in more than the precise number of hours of darkness necessary to sustain flowering. Tests show that up to 15 hours of darkness will proportionately increase the rate of flowering. More information on this is in the section on electric light (Chapter 2).

The critical nightlength of marijuana is important in some greenhouse growing situations such as in growing a spring crop, and is discussed in Chapter 3. It is also helpful to know the critical nightlength of certain varieties of marijuana that are exceptions to the standard 12 hours light, 12 hours darkness flowering cycle. An example of this is the variety of marijuana called William's Wonder, a very early maturing variety often grown outdoors in northern locations. Unlike most early maturing varieties, however, William's Wonder, needs very intense light to mature. Indoor growers have been disappointed with this variety under lights. If given the standard flowering cycle the buds are leafy, and yield is low. By knowing the critical nightlength of this variety growers can improve its yield under lights. This variety will take 13 1/2 hours of light a day, and still fully mature (the critical nightlength is 10 1/2 hours of darkness). If given the extra light the yield of this variety increases proportionately.

Marijuana cultivators have come up with techniques to force flowers in all kinds of growing situations, whether it be under electric lights, outdoors, or in a greenhouse. Besides looking for maximum yield, they might be trying to foil would-be thieves or avoid detection. These techniques are not usually costly or difficult.

Growers using electric lights, for example, are always using flower forcing techniques. Many of these growers, however, are not aware of the full potential of controlling the photoperiod, some of which will be examined in the following chapters.

2

electric lights

Most people who attempt to grow marijuana indoors under electric lights are aware that the light cycle has to be changed for the plants to flower. Growers use 18-24 hours of light when their plants are in vegetative growth. With a simple timing device, the light cycle can be shifted to 12 hours on, and 12 hours off. In about 2 weeks the first flowers will be mature enough to show the sex of the plant. It is as easy as that. Just keep the lights on that cycle and in 6-10 weeks the marijuana can be harvested. In terms of light, about the only thing a cultivator has to do is be sure the marijuana is kept in total darkness throughout the 12 hour "night" cycle. Stray light, from open doors or windows, will effectively keep a crop out of bloom.

Nonetheless, there are many questions concerning the flowering of marijuana under electric lights that are worth considering. Electric light gardening has gone hand in hand with other high-tech growing techniques such as the "sea of green" growing method, where the plants are closely spaced for maximum yield in the shortest amount of time.

A large indoor growing space, with 400-watt H.I.D. lights.

Hydroponic growing units of one sort or another dominate the indoor scene. (Carbon dioxide gas may also used to speed up the growth of a crop.) One can relatively easily set up a system that produces a harvest every 8-10 weeks.

All the techniques mentioned above, and even simply growing plants exclusively under electric lights, represent the "cutting edge" in terms of applied horticultural technology. These methods are being employed for growing marijuana because it is a high-value crop.

For other crops, like legal flowers or vegetables, the above techniques have to be used very judiciously, if they are to be cost-effective. If used judiciously on marijuana they make up only a small percentage of the value of the crop.

Growers don't need to purchase expensive systems to grow marijuana. Even fluorescent lights can grow decent marijuana if the crop is tailored to the output of the lights. The key here is inducing the marijuana to flower at the right time. How and when marijuana is put into flowering will largely determine how well a crop comes out, especially under lights. Every cultivator growing plants under lights controls the production of flowers. How the techniques are applied will determine how soon the harvest comes in, and also how large the electric bill will be.

Though small in relation to the value of the crop, the cost of growing under lights is significant. With electricity rates pushing $.15 per kilowatt hour (1000 watts per hour), wrong moves add up fast. With these parameters in mind we will take a look at how growers are using electric lights to grow marijuana.

The lights most often used for growing marijuana are fluorescent, metal halide and high pressure sodium bulbs. Each kind of bulb does an adequate job of growing pot.

Even with the strongest electric light, however, plants are only getting 1/8 to 1/4 the light of a sunny day outdoors in the height of summer. On a hot clear summer day outside a plant may receive up to 12,000 foot-candles of light. Indoors, under a high intensity sodium light only about 2,000-3,000 foot candles (FC) will be striking the plant.

A two-tiered fluorescent-lit system, in full bloom.

The intensity of light is measured in either foot-candles or lumens. A foot-candle is the density of light striking the inner surface of a sphere 1 foot away from a 1 candle-power source. One foot-candle equals 1 lumen per square foot.

Marijuana will grow in 800 FC of light, but not vigorously. The minimum needed for a good crop is 1500 FC. This is the intensity of light directly under a fluorescent tube.

Lower light intensities can be compensated for in a number of ways. One is that growers usually give their plants very long lighting periods, (18 -24 hours), when the plants are in vegetative growth. During flowering long lighting periods are not possible, so some growers add an extra light bulb during flowering. Surrounding the garden with reflective surfaces is another way to assure that all available light is used. Mylar, aluminum foil and white paint are commonly used on walls around the growing area.

"Sea of Green"

The other method of compensating for low light levels is by keeping plants grown under lights much smaller than full sized plants. Growers have employed what has become known as the "sea of green" method to keep yields up. With this method plants are grown spaced closely together and flowering begins when the marijuana is young.

Just how young the plants are when flower induction is employed, depends on the light. With fluorescent light mature plants should only be 18 inches high at maturity, because adequate light penetrates only this deeply into the plant canopy. Marijuana grown to maturity under fluorescents can be made to flower within 30 days of sprouting. The plants are often only 6-8 inches high when the bloom is initiated.

Under metal halide and high pressure sodium lights plants are often harvested at 3 feet or under. Again, this is because adequate light penetrates only to about this depth, especially when plants are closely spaced. Flowering is initiated when plants are 6-18 inches tall, depending on how thickly they are planted.

The grower using sodium or halide (high-intensity discharge, H.I.D.)

A "sea of green" growing unit, containing five plants per square foot. Most of these plants, when harvested, were under two feet high.

lighting has some latitude as to exactly when to initiate flowering. One grower cultivates plants at 6 inch centers (4 per square foot). His space, lit by a 1000 watt sodium light, covers 25 square feet and holds 100 plants. He has recorded yields of up to 40 ounces (1132 grams) of manicured flowers with this technique. This is a very intensive use of the "sea of green" method requiring heavy production of cuttings, automated watering, and good ventilation.

Other growers favor a less intensive use of the "sea of green" technique, as few as one plant per square foot. Here flowering is initiated when the plants reach a height of 12-18 inches. At this height the plants have begun to branch and the main stem thicken. Since the size of the terminal bud (the main flower on an unpruned plant) is related to the girth of the stem this is desirable.

With these branches, the plants also set flowers wherever there is available light. Bigger plants take slightly longer to grow, 7-14 days, but overall take much less work than the super-intensive method described above. Yields of 25 ounces (708 grams) are typical with a well run system such as this.

You can grow larger plants than those mentioned above, but once in bloom, the lower branches don't get enough light. H.I.D. light penetrates well about 3 feet into the plant canopy, but flowers further away are small, if they form at all. Essentially, if you grow larger plants, you are wasting electricity because the overall yield will not increase. (see picture next page)

One other reason a grower may want to use the less intensive, 1 plant per square foot, "sea of green" technique is legal, not horticultural.

There is no doubt that "sea of green" methods work. Be advised, however, in the United States, at least, the authorities are not giving prizes for the best growing techniques. Home growers especially may want to use the modified "sea of green" method as a means to cut back on the number of plants.

Cultivating more than 100 plants, including cuttings, is more likely to be charged as a federal offense, with mandatory sentences. The sentence for first time offenders with 100 plants is 2 years in the slammer,

A "sea of green" growing unit, with one
plant per square foot, grown from cuttings.
(See next picture for this unit in bloom.)

One plant per square foot, in bloom.
Maximum height is 2 1/2 feet.

These 4-foot plants look good; but notice the lack
of flowers on the bottom two feet.

(add about a year for each additional 100 plants). The "Feds" can also go after people with less than 100 plants but they usually let the local authorities take the small fry.

The only good news on the crime front is that the "Feds" are no longer counting each plant as 1 kilogram (2.2 pounds) of pot. Instead, unless the plants weigh more, each is charged as 100 grams. Since the typical yield of plants grown by the "sea of green" method is from 10 to 25 grams of manicured flowers, charges brought against indoor growers will still not reflect reality.

All you high roller types out there should be advised also that the latest (1995) Crime Bill mandates the death penalty for cultivating 60,000 plants or more (4th offense). In order to avoid becoming the first one on your block busted under this law, keep that plant count down.

Feeder Systems and Multiple Harvests

Some growers harvest a crop of marijuana every 2 months. They do this by setting up 2 or more different growing areas. The only requirement is that the light from one system does not enter the other. A system producing all female plants might include the following: 4 four foot long, 2 bulb fluorescent shop lights and shelving about 18 inches wide. A system like this is used for cloning (see page 75) and vegetative growth. Marijuana plants are kept in 18-24 hours of light here until they are ready for flowering. The fluorescent system described is big enough to feed a 1000 watt flowering chamber.

Fluorescent systems have some advantages over a 250 or 400 watt halide system. True, they use more electricity, but each 4 foot light can be turned off and on as needed. Fixtures with electronic ballasts save about 15% on electricity, and are much lighter and easier to move than the fluorescent lights of old. Another plus is that the fixtures are very inexpensive. The light from fluorescents is cool and less likely to burn plants. It is also spread out evenly over the length of the tubes, so a lot of plants fit under one light. The inexpensive cool white tubes produce a lot of blue light, which grows a good bushy plant up to about 18 inches in height. (Full spectrum tubes do a better job on cuttings and warm white tubes are best for flowering).

A vegetative growth space using a 400 watt metal halide light is about 4 feet by 4 feet. A 250 watt halide covers 3 feet by 3 feet adequately. Halides have a lot of blue light which is needed in vegetative growth. Cuttings also do well in this spectrum of light. High intensity lights are hot and must be kept a foot or more away from plants. Days are long in the vegetative growth chamber. The light is left on for 18-24 hours per day. The more light, the faster the growth. Walls should be lined with aluminum foil or mylar to reflect usable light back at the plants. Plants are kept here until half of them are up to 18 inches high, and then they are moved to the flowering chamber.

The flowering unit should be about 4 x 8 feet. It might have two 400 watt high intensity discharge sodium lights, or a 1000 watt sodium on a light mover. The copious amount of red light produced by these lights stimulates the production of flowers. The photoperiod in the flowering chamber is usually 12 hour light followed by 12 hours of uninterrupted darkness. When the system is turned on and off is the grower's choice. While in darkness, the flowering chamber must be totally isolated from any light sources.

One consideration as to when to run electric lights is that infrared detection devices, sometimes used by police agencies and power companies to detect high energy use (by the production of heat), are less effective in daylight hours.

A system including a vegetative and flowering area can be set up in a room only 10 x 10 feet. In such close quarters, one of the most important considerations will be making sure no light enters the flowering chamber when the light is off. Plants must also have a steady supply of fresh air, or better yet, carbon dioxide (page 75) anytime the lights are on.

The systems described above are single flowering and vegetative units. More units can easily be added in grid-like fashion. Although the sky may be the limit (in terms of adding units), the more you add the more professional you need to be. Requirements such as available electricity,

Starting units, lit with fluorescent bulbs.

A clone feeder system.

heat dissipation, odor control and available carbon dioxide often limit the size of a system at a particular location.

Another consideration for those contemplating multiple harvest systems are insect pests, which have shut many a system down. The three worst; spider mites, white flies and aphids, can be kept at bay by air movement in and around a plant. Other tips for keeping insects out include: cleaning growing areas between crops (use a cup of hydrogen peroxide in a gallon of water); filter air coming into the growing space; keep pets out of the growing area; thoroughly inspect any plant material bought into the growing area; and avoid working in your regular garden just before entering the pot garden.

Some growers have continuous yield gardens, where plants are moved into the flowering area whenever they are ready, rather than all at once. Insects can become a problem in these gardens. Because there are always plants in the flowering space, it can't be shut down and cleaned between crops. These growers often employ beneficial insects to control the predatory ones like mites. Usually beneficial insects are more helpful if the problem is discovered early on. Also, beneficial insects never really get rid of white flys and infestations tend to flare up periodically. Having a defined crop and cleaning the space between uses is a better alternative. Eliminating predatory insects is much more feasible when the plants are small or in the cutting stage because much less plant material has to be treated.

Longer Nights

The standard 12 hours on, 12 hours off, used by marijuana cultivators to flower marijuana, can be adjusted to help ripen the bloom. Fewer than 12 hours of light, once the flowers are formed, will help ripen marijuana flowers. Some growers use 13-14 hour nights for the last 4 weeks of flowering, especially when growing hard-to-ripen varieties like Thai or Cambodian marijuana.

This will help ripen flowers, but due to the fact that the flowers will be receiving less total light, the flower size may be smaller. To use this tech-

Aphids out for a stroll.

Photoperiod alteration has forced a whole new flower to grow from the end of the main stem.

Two plants treated with photoperiod alteration, at harvest.

nique effectively what really has to be done is to supply the plants with more light during the "day cycle". Growers using a 1000 watt metal halide, for example, could add a 400 watt high pressure sodium light when using these very "short days". If the cycle of long nights of 14 hours is started 4 to 5 weeks into the flowering cycle, the flowers will ripen up to 18 days sooner.

Photoperiod Interruptus

Some strains of marijuana move easily back and forth between the flowering and vegetative growth stage. These plants are usually easy to "clone", or can readily be brought back into vegetative growth, even late in the flowering cycle.

Many of these strains are tropical or hybrids of mixed tropical and temperate ancestry. Thai and Jamaican varieties, for example, are known to exhibit this trait. Many of the hybrids made between these and less tropical varieties, like Afghani, also exhibit this trait.

Cultivators using electric lights have reported being able to flower these plants 2 or even 3 times in succession without cutting back the plants. Instead of growing new plants, these growers report they can induce their plants into multiple flowering. This is done by photoperiod alteration.

The marijuana is put into flowering for 5 weeks at the standard cycle of 12 hours light, 12 hours darkness. (At this point the flowers are well defined but unripe.) Continuous light (24 hours a day) is then given to the plants for a period of 3 weeks. During this three weeks the first blooms will ripen and the plant will put out new growing shoots.

The marijuana is then once again put into the flowering cycle. This time the plant can be allowed to mature, or, if the main stem is in good shape, the cycle can be repeated.

The small plants usually grown under lights bear the biggest flower at the tip of the main stem. This is called "apical dominance". On small marijuana plants, this flower can be half the yield by weight from that plant.

For successful continuous flowering, it is necessary that the main stem regrow a hardy new shoot. With the right varieties, this technique can be very effective, yielding flowers 25-50% the size of the initial bloom.

Considering the time it would take to grow new plants for each crop this technique can save growers months.

Other alterations of the flowering cycle can also increase the weight at harvest. Even a few days of continuous light between the 4th and 5th weeks of flowering stimulate many varieties of marijuana to produce more flowers. Normally the production of new flowers has run its course by then and each calyx is just beginning to mature. The photoperiod alteration seems to reset the production of flowers, increasing the weight at harvest of some varieties by 10% or more. (Harvest time is delayed by only a week or so.) Since light and dark cycles have such a large effect on marijuana plants, alterations of the photoperiod are a fertile area for exploration.

3

multi-cropping in a greenhouse

Greenhouse flower forcing is well understood, both for marijuana and for legal flowers. The devices and materials needed are available at many greenhouse supply companies or can be obtained at most good hardware stores. Growers cultivating marijuana in greenhouses often grow off-season crops (crops that mature at times other than autumn). This is usually accomplished with flower forcing techniques, through a process that is sometimes called light deprivation. Black-out curtains are used to artificially lengthen nights, which induces the marijuana to flower.

As was mentioned in a previous chapter, greenhouse grown hemp was the subject of the first experiments to prove that some plants can be induced to flower out of season. In the case of marijuana, this can be done in two ways, with shading or without. The period when plants need no shading includes the regular autumn harvest time, but also the winter and spring months.

Flowering Freely

Marijuana will flower on its own in a greenhouse from about mid-August until mid-March the following year. (Note: in the latitudes south of the equator the times are opposite of those in the north, that is mid-February to mid-September.) The actual dates are determined by the variety of marijuana grown and the location of the greenhouse. Outside of these dates, marijuana can be induced to flower with the use of blackout shading systems, which are discussed below.

During the period from mid August until mid March marijuana grown in a greenhouse will begin to flower when very young, even at less than 3 weeks of age. Any plants put into the greenhouse during this time will immediately set flowers, unless the plants are receiving light during the night cycle. A small amount of light from a 60 watt incandescent light, for example, is enough to prevent marijuana from flowering.

Growers who are able to do a winter marijuana crop sometimes use this information to keep their marijuana from flowering, at least until the plants are large enough to give a good yield. This is easily done with a few incandescent bulbs (60 watts per 50 square feet) turned on for a few hours after dark. Since marijuana is so sensitive to light, this is enough to keep the plant from flowering. When the marijuana reaches the desired stature the lights are removed and flowering will commence.

One tip for those who grow marijuana in a window in their house: if you want your marijuana to flower during the fall and winter months, you must prevent light from reaching the plant during the night cycle. The reason plants often don't flower in a living space is they receive illumination from a light source at night. Even small nightlights are enough to interfere with flowering.

The "Green" Curtain

Sometime around the spring equinox, March 21, the days become too long for marijuana to flower in a greenhouse on its own. The exact date of when a plant will return to the vegetative cycle is determined by the latitude of the greenhouse and the variety of marijuana being grown. (See chart later in this chapter.)

The length of day and night are determined by the tilt of the earth on its axis. At the equator daylengths are fairly constant (11-14 hours) year round. The further from the equator, the greater the difference between day and night lengths in winter and summer.

Even during the long days of spring and summer marijuana can be induced to flower in a greenhouse. The secret of achieving off-season flowering in a greenhouse is to set up a shading (blackout) system to artificially lengthen nights. The shades are made of opaque material which is draped over the marijuana at specific times.

Black sheet plastic of 6 mils thickness or more is commonly used for blackout shading, but any material capable of totally cutting out incoming light will work. Nylon tarps or opaque window shades are two other materials a grower might use. Other growers have used large cardboard boxes or have a mobile crop which can be moved on wheels into an area of darkness, such as a shed.

Flower forcing by the use of light deprivation is a common technique used in the legal commercial flower industry. Because of this, many superior fabrics have been developed for use in flower forcing. Some of these fabrics are made to reflect excess heat away from developing flowers. Other fabrics are made to "breathe", allowing air to penetrate, but not light. These fabrics are available from nursery supply companies. Shading systems made specifically for flower forcing are available for many common greenhouse sizes.

A small commercially produced unit called the "Grobot" (made in Holland) has a curtain system attached to a timer. To shorten days and induce flowering all the grower has to do is set the timer, much like a grower using electric lights. The system has a motor driven shade which unfurls like a hood on a baby carriage. Most strains of marijuana will flower as soon as they are supplied with about 12 hours of continuous darkness each night. Even in the height of summer when nights are short (10 1/2 hours or less throughout the temperate zone), the Grobot can be programmed to add the needed darkness. A new, simplified model of the Grobot will soon be on the market. The Grobot proves that greenhouse flower forcing can be automated. These units can also be used outdoors and are available with solar power units.

A spring greenhouse crop. Note the blackout shades —
a crucial element for off-season cultivation.

A "Running Bud." This forced greenhouse flower received light during the night cycle, leading to both flowering and vegetative growth.

This "Grobot™" flower-forcing unit contains ten clones.

To force marijuana flowers in a greenhouse, growers are essentially striving to set up a light-tight space for their plants. Since this light-tight space must be able to open to admit light and close to simulate night, the shades are usually hung. Cable systems to which the blackout curtains can be attached are easy to make. Metal cables and devices for drawing it taut across the greenhouse, are available at many hardware stores. The curtains can be connected to the cables with anything from drapery hardware to shower curtain hooks.

Another low-tech method of shading marijuana is to set up a kind of scaffolding around the plants, and then drape the fabric over it. Any kind of pole, like bamboo or wood, can be used to make this scaffolding. This system is the easiest to set up, but takes the most work to operate.

Commercial flower-forcing systems for greenhouses are also available, but tend to be too big for most marijuana growers. Most systems still require that the shades be moved by hand. Since most commercial greenhouses are set up to be labor intensive this is not a problem. Also, a lot of things can go wrong with movable shades. (See pictures in color section)

Timers and motors that will automatically open and close drapes and curtains have just become available. Small systems use drapery curtain rods and cost from $100 to $400. These devices will open or close curtains at the precise times needed to induce flowering in marijuana. An "A" frame system with the drapery rod in the center, and the curtain suspended on cable along the sides is easy to set up. Use stationary curtains to make the system light tight. No light should enter the growing area when the curtains are closed.

The need for automated shading systems points out the downside of forcing flowers in a greenhouse, because if they are not automated, the shades have to be moved 2 times daily for 6 to 8 weeks. Every day missed has some effect on the flowering. Flowers elongate and get less dense as shading periods are missed, although one day missed per week will not wreck a crop. However, if you plan to miss a day, be sure to leave the curtains open. Days missed toward the end of the flowering cycle (the 5th to 10th week) will have less effect than early on in the flowering cycle. Some growers skip the last 2 weeks of shading, harvesting just before the plants revert to vegetative growth.

Very Long Nights

Some growers also artificially lengthen the nights to as long as 14 hours to more quickly ripen a crop. Longer nights work well in those greenhouses that get intense light during the day cycle.

Studies show that using very long nights (13-14 hrs) is most effective if used after the 4th week of flowering. In the first four weeks a cycle of 12 hours light, 12 dark is used. Flower weight is lower if very long lights are used too early in the flowering cycle. (This is primarily a ripening technique.)

Growers can reduce the time needed to mature a crop by up to 2 weeks by using longer nights. Plants exposed to 14 hour nights are also slower to return to vegetative growth. You can neglect to shade the plants at all during the last week or so of flowering with very little adverse effect. Reducing the number of weeks a crop of marijuana has to be shaded to mature makes greenhouse flower forcing a much more feasible undertaking.

Critical Nightlength and Spring Crops

In a greenhouse, cultivating a spring marijuana crop is often the favored off-season method of achieving a harvest. Growers often try to time their crops to take advantage of the naturally long nights at this time of year. Depending on when the marijuana is put in the greenhouse, shading can be totally or partially avoided.

The 2 variables here are the variety of marijuana being grown and the location of the greenhouse. Trying to match photoperiod with shading needs can be tricky but the charts below should help. The grower needs to determine what is called the "critical nightlength" of the variety of marijuana that is being grown.

For marijuana, the critical nightlength is the minimum number of hours of uninterrupted darkness needed to fully mature a plant's flowers. Outdoors, in natural growing conditions, marijuana will begin to flower in shorter nights than those needed to bring the plants to harvest. The critical nightlength is reached relatively late in the flowering cycle (6 weeks into a 9 week flowering cycle).

Both outdoor and greenhouse growers doing an unforced fall crop can easily plot the critical nightlength of a particular variety of marijuana. You need to know the date of harvest and the number of weeks the flowers took to mature. The critical nightlength occurs about 2/3 of the way into the flowering cycle. Once you have a date you need to find the length of the night on that date in your location (see chart). This is the "critical nightlength" for that variety. In terms of flower forcing, it is the minimum number of hours of uninterrupted darkness needed to fully mature the variety.

Knowing the critical nightlength is helpful in forcing a spring crop of marijuana in a greenhouse. Once the grower determines the critical nightlength of a variety, he or she can plot the date during spring when this critical night occurs (Note: the nightlengths during spring and fall are similar). After this date the marijuana will need shading to mature; otherwise the plant will begin to return to vegetative growth.

As you can see from the charts, some varieties of marijuana will flower without shading as late as the beginning of May, depending on the location. If the crop can be harvested within a week or so of this date no shading will be needed. If, on this date, the crop is still 4 weeks from harvest, 2-3 weeks of shading will be needed for best results. Once the shading is employed, long-night cycles of 12 hours or more should be used.

Shading Specs

Marijuana does not need much light to keep it from blooming. So, as a practical matter, the best time to shade is in poor light. If a crop only receives good light until 3 pm, the best time to shade is after that. Similarly, if the marijuana is not in direct sun during the early morning, this is the time to shade plants with blackout material. Shading plants in full light is risky because heat builds up under the shade material, especially if it is black plastic.

Critical Nightlength

VARIETY	CRITICAL NIGHTLENGTH	FINISH DATE (Outside-No. California)
Mexican:		
Northern states		
Guerrero	12:00	Nov. 1
Michoacan	12:00	Nov. 1
Mexican:		
Southern states		
Acapulco	12:10	Nov. 10
Oaxaca	12:25	Nov. 25
Mexican Indica Hybrids	11:50	Oct. 25
Jamaican	12:15	Nov. 15
Columbian	12:30	Dec. 1
Thai	12:40	Dec. 10
Nepalese	11:30	Oct. 15
Hindu Kush	11:30	Oct. 15
Afghani	11:20	Oct. 10
Moroccan	11:40	Oct. 20
HYBRIDS		
Jack Herer	11:30	Oct. 15
Haze	12:00	Nov. 1
Northern Lights	11:30	Oct. 15
Skunks (early)	11:30	Oct. 15
Skunk 1	12:10	Nov. 10
Shiva	11:40	Oct. 20
Early Girl	11:15	Oct. 10
Big Bud	12:00	Nov. 1
Williams Wonder	10:30	Sept. 10
Early Purple	11:30	Oct. 15
M 39	10:15	Sept. 1

Location, Location, Location

CITY AND LATITUDE	APPROXIMATE NIGHTLENGTH BY DATE:			
	3/1	4/1	4/15	5/1
Albuquerque 35°	12:13	11:22	10:58	10:16
Amsterdam 53°	13:17	12:27	10:04	9:10
Anchorage 62°	14:19	10:33	9:02	8:20
Atlanta 39°	12:21	11:27	11:00	10:18
Barcelona 43°	*same as Boston*			
Boston 43°	12:44	11:21	10:27	9:55
Calgary 53°	*same as Amsterdam*			
Chicago 43°	*same as Boston*			
Denver 39°	12:36	11:20	10:45	11:03
Detroit 43°	*same as Boston*			
Halifax 45°	12:41	11:13	10:34	9:58
Houston 30°	12:10	11:32	11:11	10:29
Indianapolis 42°	12:12	11:43	11:21	10:40
London 52°	13:17	10:27	13:04	9:10
Los Angeles 34°	12:21	11:27	11:00	10:18
Madison 44°	10:46	11:23	10:35	9:53
Miami 27°	12:01	11:34	11:20	10:38
Maui 23°	11:52	11:41	11:30	10:32
Montreal 45°	*same as Halifax*			
Moscow 56°	13:30	10:55	9:51	9:09
New Orleans 30°	12:11	11:32	11:10	10:58
Paris 44°	*same as Madison*			
SanFrancisco 38°	12:30	11:22	10:50	10:12
Toronto 44°	*same as Madison*			
Tucson 34°	*same as Los Angeles*			
Seattle 44°	*same as Madison*			
Vancouver 50°	13:22	10:59	10:12	9:30
The White House 39°	12:52	11:12	10:28	10:46

6/21	8/1	9/1	9/15	10/1	10/15
9:28	10:08	11:43	11:49	12:07	12:34
7:32	8:39	10:15	11:16	12:32	13:44
4:23	6:46	8:03	9:49	12:59	14:32
9:30	10:11	11:29	11:42	12:06	12:18
8:43	9:34	10:52	11:31	12:17	12:55
9:00	9:47	10:55	11:35	12:08	12:43
8:28	9:25	12:51	11:33	12:20	13:06
10:11	10:28	11:03	11:47	12:01	12:21
8:51	9:36	10:55	11:24	12:15	12:48
7:32	9:39	10:15	11:16	12:32	13:44
9:30	10:11	11:29	11:38	12:06	12:18
8:40	9:32	10:50	11:30	12:08	12:52
10:34	10:48	11:35	11:51	11:57	12:12
10:28	11:57	11:44	11:55	12:00	12:02
7:07	8:19	9:37	10:45	12:33	9:50
9:50	10:27	11:45	11:57	12:11	12:22
9:11	9:55	11:03	11:37	12:11	12:42
7:51	8:54	10:33	11:06	12:27	13:15
9:05	9:50	10:43	11:57	12:21	13:04

The photoperiod used to induce marijuana into flowering in greenhouses is similar to that used under electric light (12 hours of light followed by 12 hours of darkness). This will induce flowering on most varieties. However, many growers using shading give their plants extra darkness as flowering progresses. Thirteen or 14 hour nights are often used for the last 4 weeks of shading.

Whatever kind of shading system the grower decides to use, it should be built large enough. Marijuana, especially when induced to flower young, will grow considerably during the flowering cycle.

It is not unusual for forced plants to double in height during flowering. Building the system large enough to begin with will prevent the need for design modifications late in the flowering cycle when the buds are delicate. Ideally, the plants should not come in contact with shades. The shades should hang in such a way so as to not to touch the plants. If plastic is used this is especially important. Marijuana leaves leaning against plastic for long periods will become wet because the plants transpire water vapor. This can lead to mold or fungus problems.

If the marijuana is shaded when the natural light is weak, ventilation during the shading cycle can in most cases be avoided. Using fans can disturb the shading material which can then allow in light. Total darkness during the night cycle must be maintained if flower forcing is to work. If temperatures are high, try to bring them down before the shades are closed. (You can also vent once it is dark outside.) Many growers swear by the breathable fabrics that emit air but not light. That way even if a very slow fan has to be used, the fabric allows the air to flow through it, rather than blow against it.

Another consideration when choosing a shading material is the color. White or light colors, which reflect light and heat, are the choice for the outside of the curtain; dark colors are needed for inside. This is important because dark colors are not reflective. Any light that enters the shaded area will only damage the plant it hits directly. If you were to use a light color on the side toward the plants, light might be reflected around the growing area. Plastic materials with a dark and light side are available. For the low-tech approach black plastic of 6 mils or more is suitable so long as the

It looks impressive — but these massive Sativas grew into the peak of the greenhouse, where ventilation was difficult. Because of their late harvest date and the greenhouse's location (far north, where autumn sun is weak), the flowers were airy, rather than tight.

shades are not closed in direct sun. Otherwise plants can overheat and be severely damaged. Whatever material is chosen, it must be opaque – light cannot pass through it.

Why Force It

There are many reasons seasoned marijuana growers use flower forcing techniques in greenhouses. The biggest one is that without forcing crops will mature much as they would outdoors – in the fall. This is also the time the narcs and thieves seem to show up, like the swallows at Capistrano. One grower I knew refused to grow at that time of year, simply because it was too risky. He did put in a crop of fast-growing flowers and vegetables to show off to the neighbors. Greenhouse spaces are becoming common, but still arouse some curiosity. This grower planted Cannabis from January to June only, harvesting 2 crops per year by using shading and electric lights to start his plants.

Another horticulturist and pothead uses shading to mature tropical varieties of marijuana. This grower has no use for the Cannabis Indica varieties of marijuana, believing the tropical Cannabis Sativa is the only smokable form of pot. Thai, Indian, Columbian, Jamaican or even good Mexican are the seeds he plants.

Unfortunately, these varieties of marijuana are also the most difficult to grow successfully. Outdoors or in a greenhouse, without shading, the latest of these Sativas might not mature until Christmas. Many marijuana crop failures occur because these late maturing varieties are planted.

This grower applies shading starting on "Bastille Day" (July 14) each year. The light at that time of year is intense and Sativas bloom prolifically in the artificially shortened days. Since this cultivator has a shading system that opens and closes semi automatically, he gives his plants 8 weeks of long nights. He uses cycles of 2 weeks of 12 hour nights, 3 weeks of 13 hour nights, and 3 weeks of 14 hour nights. Knowledge of flower forcing techniques in the greenhouse gives growers a lot of flexibility in bringing in a crop.

☽ 4 ☉

outdoor growing tips

Most growers might think that flower forcing techniques are of little use to growers outdoors. However some knowledge about when the variety you intend to plant will mature is highly important. The further north you go, the more critical this becomes, as tropical and many tropical hybrids will not mature in northern locations.

Early attempts at outdoor marijuana cultivation in the 1970s often produced huge Sativas with not a flower on them, and a killing frost approaching. Only in the deep South, California and Hawaii did most of the seed being planted mature. At the time, most of the pot in the country was imported tropical Sativa from near the equator. Since this marijuana frequently contained seed, this is often what was planted.

Outdoor growers soon learned that seed domesticated in more northerly locations had a better chance of maturing outdoors. Initially the best seeds came from northern Mexico, but soon new varieties of marijuana seeds were pouring in from around the world. The U.S. government's pot farm in Mississippi took full advantage of the situation, in some cases buying underground seed. They grew hundreds of varieties, testing for THC content.

Today, varieties of marijuana can be found that can mature outdoors in most locations. In a way, the search for the right variety for your location is a form of flower forcing. Especially in northern areas, if the wrong seed is planted, there may be few flowers to harvest.

Reliable seed, with a known maturity date, is a must for the outdoor grower. The seed should produce a relatively uniform crop, one that matures at the about the same time with consistent quality. Cuttings of plants known to thrive in a given geographic location are much in demand, and with luck can be maintained for years. Any way you look at it the choice of what variety of marijuana to grow outdoors is critical to a good harvest.

The introduction of Cannabis Indica varieties of marijuana like Afghani and Hindu Kush is often credited with spreading outdoor marijuana cultivation throughout the United States. Many of the varieties that did best were actually hybrid crosses between Sativas and Indica, where early maturity and resistance to mold were dominant. Some of those varieties like Early Girl and early maturing "Skunks" gained national attention.

Curiously, much of the seed breeding for the outdoors is being done by growers using electric lights. In many cases the plants that do best under lights, producing big buds under the relatively low light intensities of electric lights, often also mature early outdoors. (See the breeding section in Chapter 7 for more information.)

Another tip that could be important to the outdoor grower is to start late. Most varieties of marijuana will mature at the same time outdoors whether they are started in April or June. (Grown from seed, there is no difference in when a marijuana plant flowers, once plants are 40 days old.) Plants started late are smaller, which many growers find useful in keeping the plants unnoticed. As one grower put it, "Every day they are not in the ground is one day less they can be discovered." (He transplanted 3 week old plants in mid-June.)

Direct flower forcing techniques are not out of the realm of possibility for the outdoor grower. The Grobot™ pictured on the back cover, uses an automatic blackout shading system to induce flowers in marijuana at any time. It can be used outdoors and operated with an optional 12 volt solar panel.

Another unique indoor outdoor growing unit used by a grower was a VW bus with a sunroof. This grower had an early maturing variety that he pushed to a mid-August harvest by giving it long nights. He closed the top and curtains on the side windows at specified times from the summer solstice, June 21, to August 1, also moving his mobile grow unit a few times during the season.

Shading techniques to induce flowering of marijuana planted in the ground are not unknown. Large appliance boxes such as those for refrigerators or washing machines have been used to shorten days and force flowering. Boxes work pretty well, at least until it starts to rain. The grower who tried this, like the VW cultivator, used an early maturing variety, but was only able to shade for four weeks until the boxes were unusable. His flowers were a little airy. Strangely enough the boxes didn't arouse much suspicion because they were in an inaccessible area where people dumped things.

Because of factors like wind, it is usually not as practical to use shade cloth to induce flowers outdoors as it is in a greenhouse, at least not for a whole marijuana patch. Techniques for forcing single marijuana plants outdoors are possible. One grower built a scaffolding of bamboo and hemp twine around individual plants. She next made a "plant sock" out of the breathable blackout material described in the previous chapter. The sock was loose, lightweight and both easy to put on and take off of the scaffolding around the plant. Although it took considerable work, (7 weeks of shading), the grower harvested in early summer before anyone would have thought to look for pot.

5

other factors influencing flowering

Although much of the data is pre-drug war (1973), marijuana is a much studied plant, owing to its proclivity to flower induction. Cannabis is also one of the fastest growing plants, and does well under laboratory conditions.

Uninterrupted darkness is the force that induces marijuana to flower, as we have seen. There are also a number of growing conditions and chemical agents that have an effect on the flowering or sex of Cannabis. Not all of the information concerning flower forcing affects marijuana flowering directly. Some may affect the yield of the crop, or potency of the flowers, or simply increase the number of female plants.

Sometimes these effects will be dramatic, while other times the effects are more subtle; but all will be helpful in understanding and controlling the flowering sequence.

Inventive growers have come up with some interesting possibilities as to how to make marijuana a more productive plant. New cloning solutions have been invented, as well as products that are said to influence the sex of the plant. I will try to explore all credible information, as well as folklore that many growers seem to believe. Although much of the information is proven some of the techniques described may need to be refined.

Lift Off

Marijuana is generally an easy plant to grow and it does well in any well aerated, neutral pH growing medium. If it is difficult to grow at all, it is usually just as it sprouts from seed. If the growing medium is too soggy (wet without air) at this time, the plants can be stunted permanently. Marijuana is also prone to a fungal disease called "damping off," in which the plants keel over and die just after sprouting.

Another problem often encountered when the plants are very young is a yellowing or drying of the first leaves. This is caused by the pH of the growing medium. The pH, (the acidity or alkalinity of the growing medium), must be in the neutral to slightly acid range, 6.5 on a 14 point scale, is the ideal. Lower numbers indicate acidity, higher numbers alkalinity.

Early growth, then, is very important in the lifecycle of marijuana. Getting plants through this period in top condition is also important later on when they flower. Plants that have problems early on usually have lower yields at harvest. Many times an unhealthy plant will have small and sometimes delayed flowering. As the size of the flowers is often related to the stoutness of the stem, a vigorous plant is desirable.

Cultivation Techniques

Detailed information on the cultivation of marijuana is widely available. In truth, you can grow great pot by countless different methods, whether it be passive or active hydroponics, in rockwool, polyurethane foam, or even soil. Every system has its advantages and drawbacks. Done well, it would be difficult to define the best way. Growers often employ the system that helps compensate for any weakness they may have in growing plants. A grower who often waits too long to water his or her plants might employ a system that waters the plants automatically. If a grower has had problems with potting soil, he might be motivated to try rockwool or the new "growing foam".

Healthy plant starts.

We have lift off ...   A case of "damping off."

A healthy seedling.   PH problems stunted this young plant.

See the hydroponic section in appendix A for more information on cultivation techniques.

Nutrient Content of the Growing Medium

Because it is a fast growing plant marijuana needs a steady supply of nutrients throughout its life. At least 12 nutrients, including oxygen from the air, are critical for the plant's growth. When inert hydroponic growing media, such as lava rock, are used, all the nutrients must be supplied to the plant. When soil-based media are used for cultivation there may be some nutrients contained in the medium initially, but soon the nutrients will have to be replenished.

Fertilizer mixes are sold based upon the amounts of the three main nutrients they contain. These nutrients, known as the N-P-K, are Nitrogen, Phosphorous and Potassium. (Calcium should also be on the list of primary nutrients.) Marijuana, for example, uses more calcium than potassium.

Calcium is often contained in large quantities in potting soil, and sometimes in local water supplies. For this reason it is often left out of fertilizer mixes. Since calcium deposits can lead to blockages of hydroponic spaghetti tubing, it is the nutrient most likely to be left out of hydroponic nutrient formulas. The other nutrients needed for plant growth are sulphur, iron, magnesium, boron, manganese, carbon dioxide and aluminum.

Two of these nutrients are known to affect flowering: nitrogen and phosphorous. Nitrogen, the primary nutrient plants use for growth, is negatively implicated in flowering. Overly heavy nitrogen feeding is known to delay flowering.

Marijuana needs large amounts of nitrogen during growth and as flowering begins, but overfeeding with nitrogen can lead to rank growth and weak stems. On the other hand marijuana, particularly when it is forced to flower when young, will experience a growth spurt for several weeks after flowering is initiated. Nitrogen will be needed to feed this growth since without it flower formation will be weak. Nitrogen deficiency is easy to spot: in most plants the leaf stems (petiole) turn reddish. (Note: A few varieties have naturally red leaf stems.)

This leads to the question of what the optimum nutrient mix is. Often nutrient solutions high in nitrogen such as 30-15-15 NPK are used during growth, while a 15-30-30 formula is used during the flowering stage.

Phosphorus is the nutrient most often associated with flower formation. High phosphorus levels during flowering are known to increase the size of the flowers in marijuana and many other plants. Proper nutrition during flowering, including keeping the phosphorous level high, can increase the weight of the harvest by 20% over plants low in phosphate. Nutrient mixes like 15-30-30 NPK have been used successfully by marijuana growers.

The 15-30-30 nutrient formula is favored by many growers throughout the lifecycle of marijuana. Plants grow slightly slower with this formula but the stems are thicker and the branching sites are closer on these plants compared to those fed with higher nitrogen. Stem thickness is positively associated with the size of the flower the plant sets, as we have seen.

The question of how much fertilizer to apply to plants varies widely. Fortunately, marijuana has a tolerance for extravagant feeding. Nutrient levels can be measured with a dissolved solids meter which gives a fairly accurate reading, but which reads for nitrogen more accurately than the other primary nutrients. Using a dissolved solids and a pH meter are musts for those using active hydroponic systems. Nutrient levels from 750 to as high as 3000 ppm have been used to successfully grow pot. (Note: some meters measure nutrient levels differently – to get the numbers above you add a zero to the reading.) A nutrient level of 750-1500 ppm will grow fine marijuana.

Growers can also measure nutrients by the teaspoon. Using the 15-30-30 NPK strength formula, growers report fine results using 1/2 to 1 teaspoon of fertilizer per gallon of water every time the plants are watered.

Temperature

Marijuana is indigenous to semi-tropical and tropical areas. The plant likes warm temperatures, especially when it is flowering. The optimum temperature for most varieties in bloom is 60°F (16°C) at night and 80°F (27°C) during the day. The Cannabis species, however, is very diverse. You can find varieties that will set flowers in a range of 50°F to 95°F, although these are often not the best temperatures for maximizing yield. At temperatures outside this range flower production is inhibited.

If the temperature in a growing area is outside the temperature limits, some compensation can be made. This is done by increasing the optimum temperature range. For example, if your growing system or area is dipping to 50°F at night, you can increase the daytime temperature to 85°F with some positive effect. Or, if the daytime temperature is closing in on 95°F, you might decrease the night cycle temperature to 60°F with ventilation.

Temperature is also important in the sexual differentiation of marijuana. Marijuana is a dioecious plant, meaning the male and female flowers are on separate plants. To get seed you must implant the female florescence with pollen from the male.

The temperature, especially during to early growth stages, has been shown to be important in determining the sex of marijuana. Low temperatures will increase the number of male plants while temperatures in the high end of optimum favor an increase in the number of female plants. Variances from normal of 5-10% have been noted by many growers. (Normal is 52% female plants)

Color and Intensity of Light

Many flower induction experiments have been done with electric lights of different color spectra. Light can be produced in colors ranging from infrared to ultraviolet. None of these spectra of light have proven capable of inducing flowers in the absence of long nights. However, marijuana plants exposed to certain spectra of red light may produce a few flowers indicating sex, even in long days of light. Nevertheless, a full flowering cycle will not occur under these conditions.

Light in the red spectrum is known to both stimulate and inhibit flower production in marijuana. Specifically, orange-red light of 660 millimicrons on the spectral scale will inhibit flower production. Far red light, at 735 millimicrons, is known to promote the development of flowers. Marijuana is also known to require a lot of blue light during vegetative growth. Not coincidentally, the two lights most popular for marijuana cultivation emit light high in the far red and blue spectra.

The metal halide light produces high amounts of blue light, while the high pressure sodium light produces large amounts of far red light. The halide is preferred by growers during vegetative growth and the sodium during flowering. It should be mentioned, however, that both lights produce adequate amounts of both red and blue light to satisfactorily grow marijuana.

These lights are fast being replaced by lights with modified spectra more suitable for cultivating plants. H.I.D. lights were developed for use as street lights; their use in horticulture is a secondary application. A high pressure sodium light, the most efficient grow light in terms of power use to light output, (with more blue and less orange light), is already on the market. Other advanced forms of lighting such as a sodium light activated by microwaves should soon reach the market.

Light in the far red spectrum does stimulate the production of flowers, though the correct photoperiod is still required. Production of flowers is heavier under high pressure sodium lights, for example, than with metal halides. Part of this increase is because of the efficiency of the sodium light and part is because of the spectrum of light.

Although of limited use directly in forcing flowers, tests do show that far red light can shorten the flowering cycle (time to harvest) by up to 10%. A plant that takes 10 weeks to flower will take 9 if exposed to high amounts of far red light. At present incandescent bulbs (spot lights) are the best source of this spectrum of light.

Other lights, such as fluorescent tubes, also produce adequate levels and color spectra of light for growing marijuana, under certain circumstances. Fluorescent are good for producing miniature plants (page 12) for

personal stash, or for cloning, where high light intensities are not beneficial. Fluorescent lights are also make good starter systems for marijuana to
be flowered under H.I.D. light.

More specific information on the light intensities needed for cultivating cannabis is given in Chapter 2.

Ultraviolet Light

In the research as to why marijuana produces THC and the other
psychoactive cannabinoids, the subject of ultraviolet light often comes
up. The cannabinoids are thought to be produced, at least partially, to protect the plant from ultraviolet radiation in the atmosphere. Cannabis
is indigenous to mountainous areas, which receive more ultraviolet light
because of the thinner atmosphere at higher elevations. At sea level
ultraviolet radiation is filtered out of the sunlight by the ozone layer and
dust in atmosphere. Preliminary research suggests that ultraviolet light can
significantly increase the cannabinoid content of marijuana compared to
untreated plants.

Exactly how much UV light is optimum, however, has not yet been
worked out. Marijuana is thought to be indigenous to foothill areas with
elevations of 1500-2500 feet. Many experienced outdoor growers will
tell you pot grown at these elevations will be the most potent – up to
20% more potent than the same variety grown at sea level. Higher locations may be even more advantageous but other outdoor growing conditions, such as cold weather, can easily negate any advantages to the
thin atmosphere and high ultraviolet light levels.

Like carbon dioxide levels, the amount of UV radiation in the
atmosphere is increasing, in some areas dramatically. This is because
of the thinning of the ozone layer, which is allowing more UV light
to penetrate the atmosphere. In addition to a general thinning, holes
have developed in some parts of the ozone layer allowing heavy UV
penetration to the landmasses below. In short, lack of UV light
is not likely to be a problem for outdoor marijuana cultivators, even
at sea level.

High intensity discharge (H.I.D.) lights like the metal halide and high intensity sodium lights, both emit a fair amount of ultraviolet light. However, this wavelength of light is filtered out by the thick glass of the bulb, and very little reaches the plant. Most greenhouse coverings like glass and plastic films also filter out UV radiation from the sun.

If you want to experiment in this area, lights emitting UV radiation (you need UV-b producing lights) are easy to come by. They are used for tanning the body. Since this kind of tanning was a fad that went out of style, much used equipment is available. Personal tanning lights are also easily available.

Growers use two or more 20 minute ultraviolet light treatments during the day cycle. Most UV lights have timing units which turn them on for a set amount of time. This is to prevent overexposure (sunburn). As is, these lights have to be switched on manually, but they can be modified and connected to a sequential timer to automate. Small lights (used to tan your face) will treat a small (400 watt area), while full body tanning systems can be used to treat two 1000 watt areas.

If you wish to experiment in this area, remember that this kind of radiation can be damaging to the body, particularly the eyes. It is best not to be in the growing area when the ultraviolet light is on. If you have to be in the growing area wear sunglasses that filter out UV light and a hat. The small amount of UV-b radiation these lights produce can do heady things to your marijuana. Used in moderation the technique is as safe as getting a suntan. Don't get carried away though, the object is not to get the plants to glow in the dark.

Hormones

ETHYLENE – Ethylene is a plant hormone that is known to stimulate the formation of female flowers. The increase in female flowers was first noticed by farmers who used wood smoke (which produced ethylene) in their orchards to keep down insects. Fruit trees, like marijuana, often bear male and female flowers on separate plants. Ethylene was found to be the component of the smoke which feminized these trees.

Another effect of ethylene is that it is known to hasten the ripening of both fruit and flowers. Information on that subject will be explored later in this section.

Other research, some of which was done on the Cannabis plant, confirmed the increase in female flowers, and isolated ethylene as the catalyst that caused the phenomenon. Some marijuana cultivators have reported up to 70% female plants after a seed treatment with ethylene.

Treating seeds with ethylene is easy, and you won't have to go looking for a source of the gas. Certain vegetables like cucumbers and melons exude ethylene as they ripen. To treat seeds all you have to do is keep them in plastic bag, in a warm place, with a ripening cucumber, melon or banana. (The peels alone will also work.) Treat the seeds for a week or two. As the fruits ripen they give off water as well as ethylene gas. Keep seeds in a paper envelope to absorb some of the moisture. Air out the bag every day or two and remove and replace fruit as it becomes ripe. If you keep the seeds sealed up in the plastic too long they will sprout, which can be a viable method of starting seeds if it is anticipated. It is best to treat seeds just before they are going to be grown.

If you don't mind treating the whole flowering area, another time that feminizing ethylene treatments can be given is just before a marijuana crop grown from seed is induced to flower. Spread peelings from fruit and vegetables around the growing area for 1-2 weeks before the marijuana is given the flowering photoperiod. Discontinue treatment once plants are into flowering.

Since ethylene helps to ripen flowers and fruits, growers may wonder if it would help ripen marijuana flowers. Ethylene is used to ripen some fruits, like bananas, which are usually sprayed with the hormone once they reach the location they are going to be sold. Most plants naturally produce more ethylene as their fruits or flowers ripen.

Unfortunately, the studies done with ethylene during flowering have had mostly negative effects. Flowers sprayed with ethylene will not open. If they are open already they will close. Ethylene does promote the maturity of flowers, but it seems to occur very quickly. The flowers will die prematurely, and fall from the plant, especially if the hormone is applied early in the flowering sequence. Although these studies were not done with marijuana it is safe to assume that ethylene treatments during most of the flowering cycle would not be effective.

A few indoor growers report positive results using ethylene treatments late in the flowering cycle on those pesky flowers that are difficult to ripen. Strains of pot mixed with Thai or other equatorial Sativa varieties are notorious for slow ripening under electric lights. Treat the growing area as described above any time after 6 weeks of flowering.

ESTROGEN – Estrogen is the ultimate female hormone that is found in animals and some plants like certain yams. Estrogen treatments of marijuana have been the subject of much speculation. There have been many reports that it increases the number of female plants in plants grown from seed.

Treatment is easy. Soak seeds overnight in a small amount of water into which has been dissolved a birth control pill or other estrogen pill. After soaking, sprout the seeds in paper towels wetted with the water from soaking. Increased ratios of female to male plants of 10% or more have been reported by numerous marijuana cultivators.

TESTOSTERONE – If estrogen is the main female hormone, testosterone is the classic male one. Patches containing the hormone have just become available, for males deficient in testosterone.

Marijuana cultivators are interested in testosterone for its potential to grow male flowers on female plants. These male flowers are needed to produce all female seeds. (See page 78) Research in this area is very preliminary. The most likely method of treatment is misting female plants just before flowering.

NAA AND IAA – Indole-3-Acetic Acid (IAA) and X-Naphthalene (NAA) are plant hormones commonly found in rooting or cloning compounds. They are known to stimulate the formation of new roots on cuttings.

These hormones are also anti-flowering agents. They are effective in pulling plants out of flowering. They are useful to marijuana cultivators in certain growing situations. These include: treating clones that were cut during flowering; plants that are "sexed" (put briefly into flowering to reveal sex and then returned to vegetative growth); rejuvenating plants after flowering. (See page 82) Several foliar treatments, at half that recommended for cuttings, are very effective in restoring vegetative growth. There have been reports that these hormones, in higher doses than recommended, stimulate flowering. Though tests were inconclusive, this seems a fertile area for research.

GIBBERELLIC ACID – Though the flowering hormone, florigen, has never been isolated, a plant hormone called gibberellic acid is known to be implicated in flowering. A few marijuana cultivators have used this hormone experimentally to see how it effects flowering.

Applications of gibberellic acid to some long-day plants induces them to flower, even if the days are short. Long-day plants are the opposite of short-day plants like marijuana. They flower as the daylength gets longer and the nights shorter.

Unfortunately, gibberellins seem to act like an anti-flowering agent in short day plants like marijuana. Sprayed on to the leaves of marijuana, the gibberellins inhibit the formation of flowers even when the plants are exposed to short days.

Gibberellins are naturally present in the leaves of the plant where the day and night length is tracked. Plants have no regulatory organs like the brain, heart or other hormone producing glands to regulate these kinds of processes. Instead, plants regulate themselves by the ebb and flow of various plant hormones and chemical agents. The length of the lighting cycle often determines how much of a hormone is produced. In the case of marijuana the hormone wanes as the nights lengthen and flowers are induced.

Since the gibberellins are implicated in the flowering response, and the response takes place in the leaves, some pot growers have done experiments, partially defoliating plants (bringing down the gibberellin levels) in an effort to get them to flower, without long nights.

Experiments have been done removing about half the digitalis (leaf blades) on the fan leaves of the plant. For example, if the plant had fan leaves with 9 digitalis, 4 were removed. Unfortunately, growers report-ed no success with these experiments. Even when these marijuana plants were given long nights, flowering was considerably delayed and yield negatively affected.

Gibberelins are sometimes sold in solutions with vitamin B1, said to prevent transplant shock and as an aid in the rooting of cuttings. These solutions should not be used on or around flowering marijuana.

Another grower tested this hormone on female marijuana plants in an attempt to produce intersexual plants, needed for the production of all female seed (page 78). Test results were inconclusive.

Due to the way gibberellic acid effectively prevents marijuana from flowering, it may be of use in rejuvenating plants that have flowered (page 82), or stimulating vegetative growth in clones cut during the flowering cycle.

Although gibberellic acid is only a piece of the flowering puzzle, it is a strong clue that science may yet come up with a flowering brew capable of initiating and sustaining the flowering cycle of marijuana no matter what the length of day or night.

Carbon Dioxide

Carbon dioxide is an odorless gas contained in small amounts in the air around us. The amount of CO_2 in the air has been going up because of the burning of hydrocarbon fuels. At present, the CO_2 level is at about 350 parts per million (ppm) in the atmosphere.

Carbon dioxide plays an integral part in the growth of plants. Plants have specially designed cells, called metaphyseal cells, on the underside of their leaves. These cells are designed to separate CO_2 from the air around the plant and draw the gas in. The leaves have small pore-like openings, called stigmata, through which the gas is drawn. Plants use CO_2 specifical-ly for growth. The carbon in CO_2 is integrated into plant tissue. By weight, dried plant material contains almost 50% carbon, all of which is derived from CO_2.

The growth of marijuana and most other plants is known to accelerate if higher than normal amounts of CO_2 are given. If you double the amount of CO_2 to 700 parts per million, many plants, including marijuana, will increase their growth rate by 50%. Many growers report up to an 80% growth increase using 1500 ppm CO_2 when marijuana is in the vegetative growth cycle.

Flowering time will not be cut in half under CO_2 enrichment but 2 weeks or more can be cut off the flowering cycle by using CO_2. A flower that takes 10 weeks to mature normally will mature in 8 weeks with CO_2. In addition, growers often report a 20% increase in flower weight on plants that have been CO_2 enriched. This is because CO_2 significantly increases the size of the stem and branches as well as flower initiation sites.

Another effect of CO_2 enrichment is that enriched plants will be vigorous at both higher and lower temperatures. This means the ideal growing range is extended about 5° to 55°F (13°C) nights to 85°F (30°C) days, from 60°F nights and 80°F days. Being able to operate at higher temperature can be quite important, especially if the grower is trying to set up a "closed system" where very little or no air is to be vented to the outside.

Carbon dioxide is also known to be effective in stimulating root growth. It is helpful when plants are being grown from cuttings (cloning). The gas quickly stimulates the formation of roots on marijuana cuttings.

Even if you don't intend to supplement your indoor growing area with CO_2, you still need to be aware of the role it plays in plant growth. This is because without a steady supply of CO_2 during the daylight hours, the growth of marijuana slows. In levels of less than 200 ppm, growth will stop.

For indoor growers low CO_2 levels are one of the primary reasons for low yields. If CO_2 enrichment is not used, ventilation becomes very important, especially if the plants are filling up the growing area.

In a closed area filled with plants and in bright light, ambient levels of CO_2 can be depleted in less than an hour.

One other known effect of carbon dioxide is that it increases the number of female plants. No hard data on this aspect of CO_2 enrichment of marijuana have been produced, but increases in the number female plants grown from seed of 5% or more has been reported from reliable sources.

Straight horticultural research on plants other than marijuana also support this finding.

See Appendix B for information on setting up a CO_2 system.

Magnified view of a capitate gland.

6

the obscure

Sugar

Experimenters have been partially successful in making certain plants flower by feeding them sugars, even in the absence of light. Florists often recommend that their customers add a teaspoon of powdered sugar to the water their flowers are put in to help bring out the flowers.

Marijuana cultivators have also reported some success in hastening the ripening of marijuana flowers by feeding them sugars.

If you want to try this, do so only during the last 2-3 weeks of flowering. The sugars help only with the ripening, not the formation of flowers. Use a tablespoon of sugar per gallon of water mixed with the other needed fertilizers. Treatments with sugar early in the flowering cycle may actually delay flowering.

Aromatherapy

Plants don't have immune systems to protect themselves from disease and pests. They do have defense systems based around the ebb and flow of chemicals within the plant. Scientists have recently found that the chemical methyl salicylate triggers the immune-like response in plants.

Methyl Salicylate is contained naturally in wintergreen oil, a common ingredient in analgesic liniments. White Flower™ balm, for example, has 40% wintergreen oil. This highly aromatic oil is used by some growers to mask the smell of ripening marijuana. It may also be helpful in warding off insects and disease. Avoid getting this oil on your skin or near your eyes. It is for external use only.

Salicylate is also the base for aspirin. Some growers have been using aspirin or willow bark teas for cloning plants with reported success. Two aspirin in a quart (liter) of water may have the same effect as wintergreen oil when sprayed on plants.

Polyploids

Polyploidy is both the naturally occurring and induced mutation of the genetic make up of a plant. There are numerous forms of polyploids. All have differing numbers of chromosomes than the normal diploid plant. Diploids have 2 sets of chromosomes. Marijuana has 2 sets of 10 chromosomes or 20 chromosomes. These chromosomes carry genetic information which is mixed and formed into new sets when the plants are mated.

Some of the forms of polyploids are monoploid, 1 set of chromosomes; triploid, 3 sets of chromosomes; or tetraploid, 4 sets of chromosomes. Up to 8 sets of chromosomes (octoploids) are possessed by some plants, like certain varieties of wheat. The diversity of forms is one of the things that make creation of a useful polyploid so uncertain. You never really know what kind of polyploid a treatment may produce.

There are also other forms of polyploidy called aneuploids, which have differing numbers in the chromosome sets. If one of the 10 chromosome sets in marijuana contained 9 chromosomes, for example, the plant would be called a monosomic aneuploid. If it had 11 chromosomes in one set it would be a trisomic aneuploid.

Most forms of polyploids are highly unstable genetically, at least initially. Polyploids with odd numbers of sets of chromosomes are usually sterile, as are the aneuploids. The chromosomes need to be paired in mating and even a single chromosome without a mate can cause sterility or worse. In many cases it is lethal to a plant.

Polyploids are of interest to the horticulturalist because even though they are a form of mutation, a high number of both cultivated and wild plants are polyploids. More than one third of both cultivated and wild plants are thought to be polyploids. Mutation, although frequently apparently useless, does drive evolution. Through probability and chance some mutant forms bestow an advantage over the normal forms of a species. For example, many polyploids are much higher yielding than their diploid counterparts. Some common plants that are polyploids are bananas, sugar cane, coffee, potato, some apples, tobacco, and peanuts.

Over time polyploids' erratic reproduction potential equalizes, with those containing even numbers of chromosomes sets often making viable seed, much like diploids.

Polyploids hold interest for the marijuana cultivator because of the work of H.E. Warmke in the 1940s. At that time it was found that the chemical colchicine, derived from the common autumn crocus, could induce polyploidy in diploid plants. Due to the high number of polyploids found among high yielding cultivated plants, it was thought that plants with greatly increased yields could be created through induced polyploidy. Warmke made the claim that the triploid and tetraploid marijuana he created was twice as potent as it's diploid counterpart. (He used extracts of the plants in measured amounts to kill fish, and to gauge the potency of the extract.) Later reports alleged that you could double the size of the terminal bud (the flower at the tip of the main stem) by doubling the number of chromosome sets (tetraploid). Actually, the triploid form, although seed sterile, tends to produce the largest plants in most species. A triploid Cannabis plant could be propagated by cuttings.

Commercial horticulture with all its resources has produced very slim pickings despite all the work that has been done with polyploids. The seedless watermelon and a few ornamental plants seem to be the extent of the new introductions. Some of this is because of the exacting standards and uniformity that commercial agriculture demands. Also, polyploid variants often can't be grown in the vicinity of normal diploid varieties of the same plant, because the effects of cross-pollination can be negative.

Marijuana cultivators who are not intimidated by the above can have a go at creating their own mutant varieties. Who knows? You could get lucky.

Marijuana seeds can be treated with colchicine by soaking them overnight in a 1% solution of colchicine in water. Colchicine is both a poison and mutagenic, even though it is widely used by all kinds of plant breeders. A very small amount is needed to treat seed, so don't mix up any more than you need. Keep it off your skin and away from your mouth and eyes. Colchicine is not easy to get except by certified breeders. (The chemical is also used as a drug in the treatment of gout.)

As was mentioned, the autumn crocus (Colchicum Autumnal) is the source of the chemical colchicine. As very small amounts of colchicine are needed, 1% for seed treatment, and .05% for treatment of growing tips, the chemical can easily be derived directly by crushing the crocus bulbs. The liquid can be pressed from the bulbs with a garlic press. Seeds are soaked in the liquid overnight and then sprouted. To treat the seeds, they only have to be moistened, so a very small amount of liquid is needed. High die-off rates are expected on seeds treated with colchicine. About 10% of the treated seed is expected to germinate if the treatment is effective.

Treating growing tips is also relatively easy. Dilute the crocus juice with at least an equal part of water. A drop of lanolin in the solution is also helpful. Cotton swabs are moistened with the solution and placed over the growing tip. Treatment is usually for one or two days. Longer treatments are said to induce more divisions of the chromosomes but are also more likely to damage the plant. Though an organic source of colchicine, the autumn crocus should be used with caution. Do not get the juice on your skin, in your eyes, or anywhere else on your body. Don't breathe the vapors. Use gloves, tweezers, glasses and other protection to avoid contact. Some alteration of the leaves should be seen if the treatment works.

One grower who treated marijuana seeds with colchicine reported abnormalities in leaf structure, sterility, and not much else. A recent photo in the "Ask Ed" column in *High Times* pictured a polyploid strain of marijuana with variegated leaves that were hard to identify as pot. No mention was made of the plants' viability. Breeders who use this chemical in the legal flower industry may have thousands of plants to work with. It may take that many marijuana plants to find the one that stands alone.

There is some question as to whether seed treated with colchicine produces poisonous plant material. It has been suggested by some authors that the plant material should not be smoked until the second generation. There is no doubt that colchicine is poisonous: however a small amount is used, and poisons tend to break down. Most likely, the idea that seeds treated with colchicine produces poisonous material probably comes from the fact that in the legal commercial plant industry this chemical is often sprayed directly on plants. This kind of treatment definitely would make plants unsafe to use.

Treatment of marijuana seeds with colchicine is probably no more dangerous than the fungicide treatment many growers use to prevent damping off.

Once a polyploid is made the question becomes what to do with it. Can the plant be propagated? Will it make viable seed? Is it any better than the variety from which it is created? Growers should propagate the plant by cloning until it is ascertained whether the marijuana can make viable seed. Besides sterility, another problem in trying to breed polyploid marijuana is a lack of plants of both sexes. Even where male and female polyploid plants are available they often have differing forms that make them unsuitable for making viable seed. Crosses between polyploid and diploid marijuana are possible and have as much chance of success for breeding purposes as crossing two polyploids. Expect a wild seedline, with high variability, if you succeed.

The many generations it takes to get a polyploid into an advantageous, usable form is not all that long when some growers are harvesting an indoor crop every month. Since the terminal bud, the flower at the tip of the main stem, is often the part of the plant most effected by polyploidy,

Clones grown in a tropical fish tank.

marijuana remains a likely candidate for success as a polyploid.

Other methods are said to occasionally produce polyploids. Severe and continual defoliation occasionally produce polyploids as vegetative growth returns. Strange growth patterns on "mother plants" that are cut back on a regular basis could indicate that some mutation is taking place. Very short daylight cycles (8 hours or less) are said to occasionally produce polyploids in short-day plants like marijuana.

Good Clones Never Die

Clones are cuttings taken from the growing tips of marijuana plants. The cuttings are then prodded to grow new roots. A new plant, genetically the same as the plant from which the clone was cut, is produced. Cloning is an easy method of growing an all female crop.

Having all female plants cuts down by half on the number of plants needed to grow a crop compared to one grown from untreated seed. In addition, only the best female plants would be perpetuated. After a few crops all the marijuana plants will be the heartiest female.

Cloning can be tricky, especially if the marijuana is flowering when the cuttings are taken. The cuttings are delicate and need pretty exacting standards of warmth, humidity, and aeration. As usual there are one hundred and one ways of making clones. In summer you might root a few cuttings in a jar of water. Small rockwool cubes are used by many growers who need large numbers of clones. Peat cubes that expand when watered also work well if they are pH neutral.

For an easy, automated method of rooting cuttings – think fish. Tropical fish, that is. The tank and equipment needed to keep tropical fish are ideal for rooting clones. A ten gallon tank (up to 60 clones) with heater and aerator can be bought for less than $50.00. These systems produce everything the cuttings need – heat, humidity and aerated warm water. Set up the tank, add some rooting compound with fungicide, a touch of fertilizer, and set the lights for vegetative growth.

Clones usually die out for two reasons – viruses and old mother plants. Although marijuana is an annual plant, it does behave like a short-lived

During the summer, cuttings will
sprout roots just about anywhere.

A tropical fish tank with 60 cuttings. The styrofoam is broken off when the seedlings are ready for planting.

perennial if it is always kept in the vegetative growth cycle. These are called "mother plants", and the clones, or cuttings, are taken from them. Marijuana will survive for up to a couple of years like this. Eventually, however, the "mother plant" will die off as its interior phloem, or sap system, becomes clogged and the plant is no longer able to deliver sap to the branches.

Although the original plant may die there is no reason for the clone not to continue. Since the cuttings are taken from new growing tips a new "mother plant" can be started which will last as long as the original. The continuous cutting-back to get clones also helps to shorten the life of the "mother plant", although as an annual it has a limited life cycle in any case. Mother plants often die quickly and unexpectedly so it is good to change plants frequently.

Many marijuana cultivators don't keep "mother plants". They take cuttings from the bottom of plants just before they are induced to flower. If you are confidant of your cloning technique this is a good way to go, and it avoids the fatigued "mother plant" syndrome. You might want to hold back a plant or two in case, for some reason, the cuttings don't take root. Taking the small lower branches of plants for clones actually increases the yield on the upper branches when these plants are flowered.

Clones often begin to run down after catching a virus. Viruses are insidious and impossible to get rid of but usually slow to come on. Insects like spider mites and white flies are vectors for viruses. Viral diseases often take hold after a severe insect infestation and no treatments are available. Most viruses don't kill, they just sap a clone's vigor. The clones don't die, they just sort of fade away. Viruses are often not transmitted through seeds, so this may be the only way to shake this bug.

Breeding All Female Seeds

It is relatively easy to get an all-female crop by rooting cuttings from female plants. This works well for marijuana cultivators doing successive crops, or those who have access to cuttings.

For most growers, seed will be needed at some time or another. The problem is that even under good growing conditions only about 52% of seed sown will be female, on average.

A few growing factors are known to stimulate the production of female plants. In warm temperatures, for example, more females (5%) will be produced. Marijuana plants that are induced to flower when young will also yield a slightly higher number of females. Hormone treatments with ethylene (page 61) and estrogen (page 63) produce a significantly higher percentage of female plants than normal (60-70%) but still not all female.

Cultivators have long searched for a method of producing seed that will grow all female plants. Because the sexuality of marijuana is somewhat fluid and intersexes frequent (plants having both male and female flowers), hermaphrodite plants became candidates for research in this area. It has been proven that male flowers which form on primarily female plants do not impart the Y (male) chromosome. Female flowers pollinated with these male flowers will indeed produce seed that will grow all female plants.

The trick here is to gather the pollen from plants with only very slight hermaphroditic tendencies. Otherwise highly intersexual plants might be produced. Many of the popular indoor varieties like Skunk 1 and Shiva are slightly intersexual. Pollen from these stray male flowers can be helped to fertilize the female flowers around which they form, or it can be gathered and spread on a different female plant.

Gathering pollen from single male flowers is a bit tedious but can be done with a sucking device. A lens cleaning brush for cameras which is squeezed to blow air and debris from the lens can be used for this. Take the brush off the end, press the pouch to push out the air and hold, placing the brush end of the unit just above the male flower. As you release the pressure on the rubber pouch it will draw the pollen into the unit. Press the pouch to release the pollen over the flowers you want fertilized.

Seed produced by this method will yield all female plants. Although the plants are all female they will not necessarily be great plants. Some growers also report that the tendency towards male flowers builds up over time, in the offspring. Instead of a stray male flower, there are enough to light-

Male.

The first flowers form along the main stem and reveal the sex of the plant. The male has characteristic pollen sacks, the female has a fresh white pistil (for receiving male pollen), and the intersexual flower has both.

Female.

Hermaphrodite.

ly seed the plant. Again, this technique is best used on marijuana with very slight tendency to hermaphrodism.

To avoid the tendency towards hermaphrodism some growers are investigating inducing male flowers on female plants that don't have the intersexual tendency. Treatments with testosterone (page 63) and willow (aspirin) are being tested.

Double Budding

When using electric lights for growing marijuana, successive cycles of flowering can be induced on some plants. This is done with a technique one grower dubbed "photoperiod interruptus" – the flowering cycle is interrupted and the plants returned to vegetative growth after the flowers form but before they ripen.

Some varieties of marijuana respond to this alteration of the photoperiod by growing another set of flowers. The first blooms, although immature when the lights were reset for vegetative growth (18-24 hours), still matured even in the long days. New growing tips are formed while the plant is in the second vegetative cycle. From these growing tips new buds will form once the flowering cycle is restored. If the main stem can be restored to growth, a flower nearly the size of the first can be grown.

Although this technique can lengthen the flowering cycle by up to three weeks, it can also increase flower weight by 30 percent or more.

This technique is known to work well on tropical and tropical hybrids containing strains like Thai or Columbian. It should also work on any plant whose cuttings root easily. See page 27 for more details.

Rejuvenation

Marijuana is known as an annual plant. That is, the female marijuana plant blooms, sets seed and then is harvested. Successive generations of marijuana were at one time usually grown from seed.

But as growers started using cuttings for successive crops, at least a few prize plants have been kept alive for years. Growers keep these plants alive by keeping them in long days of light. These plants are usually cut back

A new flower forming, after the main
flower has blossomed.

A plant that's been cut back for regeneration after flowering.

A revived plant.

frequently to make cuttings.

Some growers revive whole crops of plants after harvest. The response of marijuana plants to revival techniques is highly variable however, and it only works well on certain varieties. A clue that a variety may respond to rejuvenation is the ease with which it can be cloned. If it's easy to clone, the variety may be easy to rejuvenate. Varieties containing some tropical Sativa are also candidates for revival. Straight Indica varieties can be difficult to bring back after harvesting.

At harvest the plants are cut back to the second branch site leaving as much leaf as possible and a few small buds. A high nitrogen nutrient formula is given to the plant. Use a photoperiod of at least 18 hours of light. Good varieties will respond with new growing tips in 1-2 weeks.

The plants that are revived are heavily branched. Plants like this are good for cuttings. If these plants are flowered they will produce many small buds. Growers reviving the whole crop should heavily prune plants to 1 or 2 growing tips for the best results.

The plant hormones indole-3-acetic acid (IAA) and x-naphthalene (NAA) are often the active ingredient in "rooting" compounds. These compounds stimulate root growth on cuttings. They have also been shown to stimulate the regrowth of marijuana after flowering. They can significantly reduce the time marijuana takes to return from flowering to vegetative growth.

These hormones help pull the plant out of flowering relatively quickly, once the vegetative light cycle is restored. Use foliar sprays several times, at half the strength used for cuttings, and treat the soil as well.

Even where it may not be possible to revive a whole crop, rejuvenation of a single plant may be advantageous. Reviving a plant that reveals itself to be great specimen only after it is well into flowering would be one example. Foliar treatments like those above make it much more likely that prize plants can be revived. Hard to rejuvenate plants can take up to 5 weeks. Once back in vegetative growth cuttings can be used to propagate the marijuana.

Be careful in using "rooting hormones". These chemical agents have been shown to suppress and delay the flowering response in Cannabis. They should not be used around plants that are about to be induced to flower.

Pollinating a female plant.

7

breeding techniques

Flower forcing, as it is done under lights, offers some unique opportunities for growers interested in breeding plants. Since growers using lights and feeder systems can harvest 6 or more crops a year, breeding objectives can be realized in a short amount of time. Couple this with the potential of using the chosen "clone mother plant" over and over as the female breeding plant, with only the male being changeable, and traits can be fixed very quickly. Once satisfactory seed is produced, both the male and female plants used for propagation can be kept alive as clones, and the exact cross made over and over again.

Breeding is considered a complex art and considering the variability of marijuana this is somewhat true. For a diploid plant, (the most common kind), marijuana has a relatively high number of chromosomes (20). Since the chromosomes impart the genetic information in propagation, the high number assures a lot of variation. Since marijuana is dioecious (male and female plants) its traits can be imparted by either parent, so it is easy to see that breeding can be a tricky business.

Many of the varieties of marijuana available to growers have already been extensively crossed or are hybrids. The progeny of these kinds of seedlines are highly variable, with seed from the same group often growing very different plants. Although variety may be the spice of life, highly variable seedlines can be a problem, especially for outdoor growers in northern areas. Growers in these areas need a marijuana variety that will mature reliably at an early date.

Still, breeding can be pretty straight forward, if the grower has well-thought-out goals. The breeder has to understand what goals are obtainable with the plants and seeds available.

Breeding objectives vary in difficulty and the amount of time needed to achieve them. The easiest would be cleaning up a seed group and making the offspring somewhat uniform – a stable line of seeds. Next would be stabilizing an existing hybrid. The third most difficult would be creating a worthwhile hybrid.

Before any breeding is done the grower needs to appraise the state of the seedline in his or her possession. Beyond the quality of the pot grown from the seed, which is easy enough to evaluate, the grower should try to determine other qualities such as if the seedline is highly inbred, a new cross, or a hybrid. Often this is not apparent until several crops are grown from the seed. Traits such as the plants' leaf structure, flower size, maturity date or size of the plants are tip-offs as the state of the seedline. Uniformity indicates an inbred seedline while diversity indicates the seedline has recently been crossed.

If one criticism can be made of the efforts made by marijuana breeders, it is that the urge to cross varieties and create hybrids is being overplayed. This is partially due to the fact that almost all the underground literature on marijuana cultivation describes loss of vigor unless marijuana plants are out-bred. To some extent this is true, especially when you consider that some seedlines are started with a small sampling, or perhaps a few stray seeds found in an ounce of sinsemilla.

Nonetheless, the scientific literature actually names marijuana (hemp) as one of the few plants that do not, in most cases, suffer from inbreeding.

As mentioned earlier this is probably because of its high number of chromosomes (20), and because the plant is dioecious. Marijuana is often highly inbred in areas where it has been cultivated for centuries. Even these highly inbred lines can show a lot of variability especially in growing areas where male plants are not culled.

One of the main problems associated with inbreeding, besides a general lack of vigor, is the fixing of detrimental traits, such as high susceptibility to disease. This is a general problem with breeding, whether inbreeding or not. In fact, detrimental traits are somewhat more likely to appear in hybrids, than inbred seedlines. An unrecognized problem in an inbred seedline can come to the surface when this seed is used in a hybrid. The problem is held in check in the inbred line, probably carried on a recessive gene and manifested in few plants. When the seedline is used to make a hybrid, especially with a very dissimilar plant, the problem can surface and be fixed as a trait in the hybrid. Again, plants from seedlines with obvious or subtle problems should not be used for breeding purposes.

At the very least, there should be no great hurry in out-breeding a variety of marijuana. Seeds that can grow hardy plants with similar traits repeatedly are of at least as much value as most hybrids and crosses. The hybrids, after all, are created primarily from highly inbred pure seed lines. Inbred seedlines are easy to maintain with simple techniques, such as line breeding which is described below.

It is true that certain hybrid marijuana, in the first crosses (F1 & F2), can surpass either parent in terms of potency, earliness, or flower size and bouquet. This is not always the case, however, as most hybrid crosses don't produce better plants than the parents.

The problem with even the best hybrids is that, unless the cross is made between plants that are very similar genetically, the seedline is unstable. The awesome first generation, F1, which is homologous (all plants similar), comes apart in successive generations. The plants revert to the parental lines over successive generations, and often show even more variation than was seen in either of the parental seedlines. By the

5th generation, F5, only 40% of the plants grown from these seeds will resemble the F1, 1st generation hybrid.

Commercial breeders are prepared to deal with the 10 or more generations of selection that may be necessary to produce a stable line of seeds from a hybrid. More often though the F1 hybrid is what is marketed commercially. If the seed is unstable, and has to be purchased regularly, so much the better for the seed producer.

It should be mentioned also that this "hybrid meltdown", where there are fewer and fewer plants with the desired characteristics after the F1 generation, is often mistaken for the loss of vigor that is associated with inbreeding. A common occurrence is seeds that grow plants with differing maturity dates or lighting requirements. The plants that mature late or need intense light will probably not do well in many growing set-ups. If the plant is a hybrid, more and more of these "dogs" will turn up in successive generations easily leading to the conclusion that the seed line is running down. Growers who cross these plants with another variety will unwittingly be creating even more diversity in the seedline, although the cross might initially produce uniform progeny. Another tip-off that you are dealing with a hybrid rather than inbred seeds are plants with differing leaf structures (some plants have wide leaf blades, others thin).

Hybrid plants are a benefit to the marijuana seed breeder. Since the hybrids are usually unstable except in the first, F1, generation, unless the plant is cloned, seed has to be continually purchased. The breeder, on the other hand, can clone both parents and continually produce the hybrid seed. But then again, so can you.

The relative importance of pure seedlines, sometimes called "heirloom" varieties, and hybrid seedlines is being debated throughout the field of horticulture. Though you can't have hybrids without the pure seedlines to breed them from, both plant forms have merits. For the marijuana cultivator, recognizing the state of the seedline which he or she is in possession of is the first step in successfully breeding marijuana.

Breeding with Clones

The secret to quickly stabilizing a hybrid or lessening the variability of a seedline is to use a single female plant, maintained through cuttings, for several generations of breeding. The female chosen for cuttings should be the best specimen available from the variety being grown. A plant as good as that chosen for cloning may show up infrequently in plants grown from seed. This is a good reason to propagate this plant.

Using the same female plant in breeding cuts down on variability because only the male plant changes. Relative uniformity can be achieved in just a few generations with most of the female progeny closely resembling the cloned female "mother plant". Once the desired level of uniformity is achieved, more typical breeding techniques can be used to maintain the seedline.

Cleaning Up the Seed Line

Growers, especially outdoor growers, often start plants from seeds unless they operate an indoor growing area, or have access to cuttings. Stable seed lines, that produce similar plants, are desirable because harvest and sexing (pulling males) times will be similar. Guerilla growers often have their own seedline which is often inbred over time.

If you are in possession of a relatively stable seed group, (the plants are 70% or more alike), you might want to do one of a few things:

1. Hold the line stable as is.

2. Spread a desirable trait to more of the seed line.

3. Get rid of an undesirable trait.

Holding this seed line as-is can be done for quite a few generations (10 or more), so if you like the variety you are growing, keep it. One easy way to do this is by a process called line breeding. Instead of picking one female to produce seed, several female plants are selected (five or more). Only a small portion of the female flowers on each plant are pollinated. If the seedline is known to be very inbred, you can also select more than one male plant from which to collect pollen. At harvest the seed is mixed and planted.

By using several plants to produce seed and/or pollen, any diversity in the seedline is preserved. A stable seedline can be kept for many generations by line breeding.

If the seedline seems stable but a few plants stand out of each crop for some desirable trait (such as maturing considerably earlier than other plants, having much larger flowers, or being very potent) the grower can play it one of two ways. The slow method is to breed only with the plants exhibiting the desired characteristics. The fast method is to clone the desirable female and breed with it until most of the female plants resemble it.

If growers want to get rid of an undesirable trait they should never breed with marijuana plants exhibiting the trait. Some of these undesirable traits may not be easy to see early in the lifecycle of the plant. An example of this would be susceptibility to mold, which is often not seen until late in the flowering stage. If you are using the line breeding method it is easy enough to discard any seed produced on plants that turn out to be susceptible. This is good reason not to breed with a single female unless you are very familiar with the seedline.

Pollinating Plants

Once the plants are selected for breeding, inseminating females with male pollen is a simple "bird and bee" type affair. Nonetheless, the procedure should be done outside the main growing area and away from fans or air currents, which could carry the pollen into the flowering area. Male plants should also kept out of the main flowering area while their flowers mature. The grower wants to avoid accidentally pollinating the whole crop, which greatly decreases its value. Male pollen is a fine yellowish dust and only a single grain is needed to fertilize a female flower. Collect and use this pollen with caution.

Females flowers are pollinated about half way through the flowering cycle, once the flowers are fully formed and just beginning to mature. The pistil, the usually white hair extending out of each flower calyx, should be turgid and fresh.

Pollen can be spread on individual female flowers with a soft artists' brush. Often only a few flowers on the lower branches of the plant need be fertilized. Even a small plant can produce hundreds of seeds if fully pollinated. Once pollinated, the females should be left outside the flowering room for a day, while fertilization takes place. Female flowers actively move the pollen in towards the center of the flower, where it is fertilized. The pollen is moved on hair-like cilia whose rhythmic waving movement draw in the pollen to the flowers' center. The deed is done in a couple of hours and a seed begins to be formed. Gently shake any unused male pollen off the female plant the next day. Female plants that have only a few pollinated flowers can be returned to the flowering area then, but the pollen is active for up to five days. They should be placed away from fans and air currents. Fully pollinated plants should remain outside the growing area for 5 days so a small alternate flowering area is needed for these plants.

Male plants die quickly after releasing their pollen, but unless there is a reason to keep them around they are usually killed soon after pollination. Dispose of male plants and their pollen carefully. If you want to store pollen it will keep at least six months in the freezer.

Seeds take 3-5 weeks to mature, at which time they often split the flower bract in which they grow. Colors from grey to brown indicate maturity. Marijuana seed is relatively short lived and can be hard to germinate after only a few years. Store the seed in the refrigerator in a vacuum sealed container for best results.

Pity the Poor Males

Male plants, once distinguished, often meet a quick death at the hands of marijuana cultivators. Many growers are more interested in preventing accidental pollination rather than breeding. Still, qualities like the size and quickness of flowering, or the robustness of a plant, are easy enough to distinguish on males and quite important in breeding. The potency of the males can be discerned by smoking or eating some of the leaf, which is similar in potency to the leaf on the females. Other traits, such as scent, are more subtle on male plants.

If you are ever going to let male plants hang out for awhile, during breeding is the time. Grow as many males as possible for breeding since males show as much diversity as the females. The more plants you have to choose from, the more likely you are to find a male that stands out. The pollen sacs on males do not usually begin opening until 3-4 weeks into the flowering cycle. By that time the determination as to the quality of a plant can be made and the losers eliminated. As with the females, choose one or more males for breeding purposes. If you are looking to keep the pure seedline from becoming inbred, breed with several males. If you are looking for less variation in the seedline, use a single male.

After 4 weeks of the flowering light cycle (12 hours light, 12 hours dark) male flowers will mature in light cycles of any length.

Quick Method of Stabilizing Hybrids

The use of cuttings, "clones" makes it easy to fix traits in marijuana, even in seedlines that are highly variable, such as in the later crosses of hybrid plants. Many growers are familiar with this scenario. The same seed group produces plants that vary widely. Some plants may look like Sativas, some like Indicas, some may be tall, some short and some in between. Needless to say, the flowers are quite different, and mature at different times.

Often times these seedlines once grew some great plants. The question is, are there still some great plants in each group of plants planted from this seed? If the answer is no, you may want to jettison this seed group and start over. If, on the other hand, the seedline still produces some choice plants along with all the variability, there are two methods of producing a stable seedline containing mostly choice plants from these unstable hybrids.

This is achieved with a method called backcrossing. When speaking of hybrids, a backcross is successively crossing back seed from an early generation of the hybrid with the seed produced from subsequent crosses. For example, a F2 (2nd generation) female hybrid marijuana plant is crossed with an F2 male. The seed produced is the F3 generation. The F2 seed and F3 seed are planted again. A female plant from the F2 group is

A male plant in bloom.

crossed with an F3 male. In each new generation (F4, F5, F6...) a male is selected and crossed back to a female grown from F2 seed.

Commercial breeders use the backcross to stabilize hybrids or highly variable seedlines. Marijuana breeders can also use this method to stabilize a hybrid. Backcrossing is effective in stabilizing hybrids but may take 10 generations.

Since marijuana cultivators often asexually propagate their best plants by "cloning" or rooting cuttings, a modified backcross continually using these "mother plants" is easy, and quickly stabilizes hybrids and erratic seed lines. In this technique a male is selected from each new generation of seed, and crossed back to female plants started from cuttings.

This plant, which is often referred to as the "mother plant" (or "goddess") is an important selection especially in this breeding situation where only the male plant will change. This technique will stabilize seedlines rapidly (3-4 generations). The females of this seedline will uniformly resemble the "mother plant" especially if good males are chosen. One potential downside of this form of inbreeding is that any problems with the "mother plant" can be imparted to the seedline as well.

If the "mother plant" has a tendency to androgyny (hermaphrodite) or a susceptibility to mold, for example, expect the same in the progeny. It's not the inbreeding that is the culprit, it's the wrong choice in the selection of the "mother plant". Backcrossing using cuttings from a single "mother plant" is much more likely to be successful if the plant is of known high quality. Ideally, the plant has been selected as the best from a large sample of females of that seedline and grown for several crops before it is crossed.

Once a stable seed line is achieved, techniques such as line breeding, described above, can be used to keep some variation in the seedline.

Hybrids & Crosses

The last step in breeding is to cross-breed two stable seedlines to create a new cross or hybrid. A cross is usually defined as interbreeding two genetically similar seedlines. A hybrid is a cross between two dissimilar lines of plants. A cross is more likely to produce a stable seedline that will breed true, but this is not by any means always the case. The union of two Indica seedlines that originate in Afghanistan, for example, have a decent chance of producing a stable line of offspring. A cross between Afgani and Pakistani seeds also has a pretty good chance of stability, if the plants are similar. A more questionable cross, and one that is more likely to produce a hybrid, would be a cross between an Afgani Indica and one from Morocco or Nepal.

Hybrid seeds, except in rare cases, are only stable (uniform) in the first generation. The first generation hybrid cross (F1) produces seed that will grow plants with similar traits, a mix of those found in the parents. A hybrid from an early maturing plant with small flowers and a late maturing plant with big buds will most likely produce a hybrid line that matures midway between early and late and has medium size flowers. Of course, you could get lucky and get an early maturing plant with huge flowers. Either way, subsequent generations of this seed will begin growing plants similar to either of the parental seedlines. The F2 generation will contain about 85% hybrids like the F1s, the rest will look like either parent. By the 4th generation only about 50-60% of the plants will be like the F1s.

Though hybrid seeds are unstable, this does not have to be a problem. A grower has a "Skunk" strain and a "Shiva" strain, for example. He crosses the plants to make a hybrid. As we have seen, over generations this seedline will grow plants like the two parents and like the hybrid cross. In this case even though the seedline is mixed all the offspring are of superior quality. It may be difficult to predict how many plants of each type you will get per crop, but to some growers, especially those growing indoors for stash, diversity is not unwelcome.

Exactly how unstable a hybrid seedline will be is in large part determined by how different the seedlines used to make it are. A cross between plants of the Indica and Sativa varieties, for example, almost guarantee a very unstable hybrid.

Crossing plants is always tricky, but it is easier to predict results if two superior lines of seeds are used. Breeding to try to make up for some deficit in a seedline, such as a variety with huge flowers but a low grade high, is trickier still. Usually, the bigger the trick the more diligence it will take to create your dream seedline. Persistence and a sense of what is achievable are valuable traits in the breeding of marijuana. With flower forcing and a quick turnover of crops what is possible is soon learned.

A novel hybrid is usually produced by crossing two varieties of fine marijuana. The best plants from the chosen seedlines should be the only plants used for breeding. Once the selection of parents is made, cuttings from each parent should be taken so that the cross can be repeated if the hybrid is all that was hoped for.

Most growers are looking for the same qualities in a seedline – early maturing, huge, potent buds that grow in low light and are insect and disease resistant. Looking forward to legalization, other growers may be trying for varieties high in cannabinoids other than delta 9 THC. For example, two cannabinoids thought to have strong medical potential are delta 6 THC and CBD, cannabidiol. Hemp (fiber) varieties of cannabis often contain high amounts CBD and little THC. Certain varieties of this "rope dope" may turn out to have very potent medical qualities. Delta 6 THC is a cannabinoid in marijuana being looked at with interest by both connoisseurs and those with a medical interest in the plant. This cannabinoid is usually found in small quantities compared to delta 9 THC, but plants high in delta 6 are known to exist, and are said to have an exotic effect.

Breeding marijuana is a complex subject on which much is not yet known. I, in no way, wish to imply that this is the only way in which marijuana can be bred. Only that this method is substantially different than that described in current literature and deserves consideration.

Marijuana flowers in bloom.

LEFT: *This "short" fall crop, started on July 1, needed no shading.*
RIGHT: *A late start, June 15, yielded a small, unobtrusive plant.*
BELOW LEFT: *Greenhouse plants growing out of control.*
BELOW RIGHT: *Sativa varieties will mature during the summer months, given proper shading.*

ABOVE: *Valerie Corral, founder of Wo/men's Alliance for Medical Marijuana, in the WAMM Garden. The Alliance was granted non-profit status two days after passage of California's Proposition 215, which legalized the growth of marijuana for medical purposes. WAMM has developed strains of marijuana with distinct medicinal properties.*
RIGHT: *A "sea of green" indoor garden, with four plants per square foot.*
TOP LEFT: *Plants growing in a fluorescent-lit feeder system.*
LEFT: *A continuous-yield system, with plants at various stages of development.*

ABOVE: *A 280-watt fluorescent
light garden in bloom.*
TOP RIGHT: *A "sea of green"
system, with 1 plant per square
foot, using 1000-watt HPS on
a light mover.*
BELOW RIGHT: *Marijuana
flowers in bloom.*

LARGE PHOTO: *The pistil with hair-like cilia emerging from the flower's calyx. The cilia move male pollen into the ovule of the flower where fertilization takes place.*

SMALL PHOTOS: *Magnified views of the female flower's drug containing glands.*

Hydroponic system using drip irrigation.

hydroponics: an overview

Hydroponics, in one form or another, is used by most indoors and many outdoor marijuana cultivators. An easy definition of hydroponics is that it is a growing technique in which the nutrients are supplied to plants in a solution of water. Most systems also utilize growing mediums designed to hold a lot of air which stimulates root growth. Hydroponic systems run the gamut from passive systems with no moving parts, to aeroponics where the root system is automatically sprayed at periodic intervals with a water and nutrient solution. A number of the active systems, employing an electric pump, are quite similar to one another in overall operation. Some of these are ebb and flow systems, aeroponics, nutrient film technique (NFT) systems, and drip systems. These systems are available as kits from hydroponic stores, but it is easy enough to design your own. However, since the passive systems are easiest to set up we'll look at them first.

A passive hydroponic system for growing marijuana may look like a regular container garden. The best systems are designed for ease of operation, especially with regard to the intervals between watering. What makes these systems "hydroponic", besides the fact that the plants are always watered with a nutrient solution, are the growing media used and the container bottom. Growing media can be as simple as rockwool in the standard gallon growing container, which is about the right size for the 2 1/2 foot plants commonly grown under lights. Soil based systems are also easy to set up, and add some CO_2 to the growing area as they are used.

The container bottom is as important as the container itself that the plant is grown in. It should be considered a nutrient reservoir which holds extra amounts of nutrient solution. By storing this solution, the intervals between watering can be increased.

The wick system is the classic passive hydroponic system. Basically wicks, such as nylon rope, are implanted into the growing medium and used to transmit water and nutrients to the plant from the reservoir located beneath the growing container.

The problem with the traditional wick system for an intensely cultivated plant like marijuana, is that it is time consuming to set up.

Under lights a grower may easily have 50 plants, which means fifty containers with three wicks each. This gets tiring, especially when successive crops are grown.

A much easier system, the modified wick system, uses the plant's own root system to wick the water and nutrients. It is often employed by marijuana cultivators. The following are descriptions of two units, one using rockwool and the other soil-based.

Both units are made to be used with plants that will harvested at 3 feet and under. The standard 1 gallon container is the right size for plants grown to this height. Each container needs a saucer about 1 1/2 - 2 inches deep. The saucer acts as the reservoir for the system. For the soil-based system, potting soil is mixed in equal parts with medium size vermiculite. The rockwool unit uses baled rockwool, which should be conditioned for pH. The bottom of the pots are filled with 1 1/2 inches of styrofoam packing material or rocks. The rest of the container is filled with the chosen growing medium.

A drip system with rockwool slabs.

For best results rockwool needs adjustments for Ph. Rockwool is alkaline and needs to be soaked in a Ph 5 solution for 24 hours before use. When watering use fertilizer solutions at 5.6-6 Ph.

A passive hydroponic unit at work.

Nutrients and water are applied in the same way you would water any plant in a container. The big difference is in the amount of water and nutrients applied. When plants are small the units are watered thoroughly, but only a small amount is left in the saucer. As plants get larger, and the roots can be seen coming through the holes of the container, more water is given. At maximum growth, the plants are watered until the saucer fills. At the end of the flowering cycle – the last 3 weeks when new growth slows significantly – once again, less of the nutrient solution is given to the plants. The plants are watered only enough to saturate the medium, with very little running out into the saucer.

Systems like this are easy to use so long as you follow the cyclic nature of how much water must be applied. The big advantage to the modified wick system is the intervals between watering; plants need to be watered about twice a week in this system. It is also easy to know if the system is working right because if too much water is being given the units will begin to smell as a slight anaerobic condition will be set up.

Although most growers who use this technique water by hand, these units can also be automated with drip irrigation. Gravity flow systems, with reservoirs (10 gallon plastic container) and spaghetti tubing to each plant are also easy to set up. Hand water the plants to find out how much water the system is using. The next time the plants need watering pour this amount of nutrient solution into the reservoir.

Active Hydroponics

Most active hydroponic units employ an electric pump, which is controlled by an electric timer. The pump moves water and nutrients from a reservoir through a feeder line and to the plants. Most often excess water is recirculated back into the reservoir, to be used again.

One-way systems, in which the water and nutrients are used only once with any excess discarded, are also in use. These systems have some advantages over recirculating systems. They need fewer adjustments to the nutrient solution both for fertilizer content and pH levels. It is also less likely that the feeder lines will become clogged with debris, as sometimes

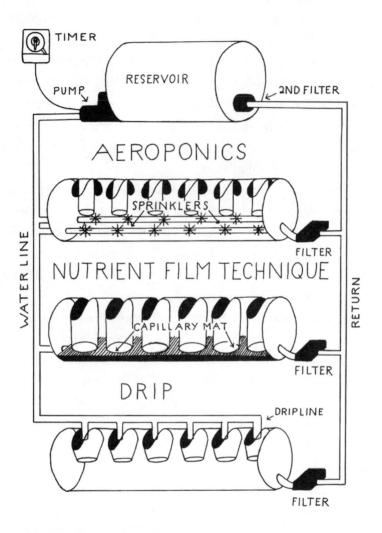

This illustration shows the various kinds of active hydroponic units: Aeroponics, which uses misters; NFT with capillary mats; and Drip, with spaghetti tubing going to each pot.

happens with recirculating systems. One way systems can get expensive if water and nutrients are applied excessively. If the excess is dumped into a drain, the systems also contribute to water pollution. One-way systems don't have to be polluting.

These systems are best when used with a growing medium that holds some water, like rockwool or polyurethane slabs, or even with the containers described in the passive hydroponic section above. If the water is applied judiciously, there is very little run-off, and what there is can be used on other plants. One grower, for example, uses a growing medium of ceramic "rocks" (which are made to hold some water) mixed with 25% perlite. This system comes on for only 1 minute three times per day so there is very little excess nutrient solution to deal with.

Most one-way systems use a large feeder line from the reservoir and then spaghetti tubing off the main line to each individual plant. Drip emitters can also be used, but are often not because they have a tendency to clog up. Leaving the emitters off is not a problem unless you have an overly strong pump.

Recirculating systems are needed when growing media that hold a lot of air, but need frequent watering, are employed. The systems might use a medium such as volcanic or ceramic rock, or no medium at all, with the plant being held in place with just a support collar. Many drip systems also recirculate the nutrient solution, but it is less necessary when the medium holds some water, such as those described above.

Recirculating systems are similar to each other in many respects. All have reservoirs and use specially designed pumps (controlled by a timer) to deliver the nutrient solution. They also have a system to return excess water and nutrients to the reservoir for further use. The difference in the systems is in how the nutrient solution is delivered to the plants. The diagrams that follow will help cultivators see what is available.

Nutrient film (NFT) systems come in many configurations. All use capillary mats which are specially designed to wick the water to plants. The water and nutrients are pumped to troughs, which are mounted at a slight downhill angle and covered with the matting. The water runs down the

A "sea of green" unit, with capillary
mats and rockwool.

matting on which the plants sit, supported by a collar or sometimes in a small container with large openings on the bottom, or rockwool cubes. Excess water is filtered and returned to the reservoir. Plants grow quickly in systems such as these because of the amount of air the roots are exposed to and the abundance of water and nutrients. NFT systems are dependable because small gauge piping, like spaghetti tubing, is not needed, so there is less chance for clogging.

In aeroponic systems the plants are held in place by a support collar and tethered at regular intervals along what is called a growth chamber. This chamber is often a 6-inch diameter plastic pipe with holes at regular intervals. These pipes are sold by many hydroponic dealers but are relatively easy to make. The pipe is equipped with a feed line and a drain pipe to return excess water to the reservoir. The feed line, which runs along the bottom of the growth chamber is fitted at regular intervals with a mist nozzle that sprays the nutrient solution onto the roots of the plant. Marijuana grows very fast aeroponically, perhaps faster than in any other system. The downside is the plants have little reserves if for some reason the system stops. Some kinds of misting nozzles for these systems also have tendency to clog. Because of this, the best aeroponic systems have some redundancy of design, such as 2 misters per plant.

Before inexpensive digital timers, flood and drain systems (also called ebb and flow systems) were precarious and undependable in operation. Digital timers (about $35) changed this because the timers can program watering cycles of as little as one minute long, up to six times a day. The nutrient solution can be delivered in very precise amounts to the marijuana crop.

Flood and drain systems use a large tray to hold the plants. The trays are periodically flooded with water and nutrients from a reservoir. The solution saturates the growing medium and is then returned to the reservoir.

Growers thinking about using active hydroponic systems should consider the potential pluses and minuses of these systems. On the plus side there is rapid growth and automation, so the grower does not have to be there to water the plants. The downside is that these systems may take

Flood and drain system using rockwool cubes.

more overall maintenance than a hand-watered or simple gravity-flow system. Frequent checks are needed to see that the system is operating properly.

In general, growers should look for several things in a well-designed active hydroponic system. The first is the method of filtering water that is returned to the reservoir. This filter should be large and easy to access. The pump also has a filter on it, which can clog if debris gets into to the reservoir. Growers often discard pump filters for this reason, though it probably shortens the life of the pump. The debris includes small bits of plant roots, rockwool, or other growing media.

Good access to the reservoir is also a necessity. Often the reservoir is attached to the troughs or is placed under the growth chamber in commercially designed, ready-made hydroponic systems. This might seem like an efficient use of space until you have to get at the reservoir, which is often. The nutrient solution has to be changed frequently in recirculating systems because plants use the nutrients in the solution at different rates. The pH of the solution also needs periodic adjustments. Growers often clean and refill the reservoirs every couple of weeks to avoid potential problems. (See Nutrients page 56)

Growers should endeavor to make their hydroponic systems as accident-free as possible but should also be ready for accidents if they happen. For example, building in a system to contain water if a pipe should break makes good sense, because a flood may lead to detection. Never attach a hydroponic system to the main water line, which can deliver limitless amounts of water even if a pipe is broken.

One other prime consideration when active systems are employed is the mixing of water and electricity. The electric pumps used, for example, are often submersible, and are placed in the bottom of the reservoir. Growers should use caution in maintaining these types of pumps. If grounding is called for, never use the system on an ungrounded power line. The system should always be shut off before it is serviced. (Always remember water is a very efficient conductor of electricity.) Safety is a prime consideration if active systems are used.

A Carbon Dioxide set-up, using pure gas from a tank.

☽ b ☺

Using CO₂

Carbon dioxide systems have a dramatic effect on the growth of marijuana and are easy to set up for use under electric lights or in greenhouses. Although several sources for producing CO_2 are available, the system of choice for most indoor marijuana cultivators is to add pure CO_2 to the growing area from a tank. Carbon dioxide generators using fuel are also used by some growers during colder months when the heat these units produce is useful.

Getting Tanked

Pure carbon dioxide comes in tanks which can be rented or bought. It is the preferred method of CO_2 enrichment in use by marijuana cultivators.

Pure CO_2 wins out over fuel generators because it doesn't produce the humidity and heat the generators do. Ambient temperatures higher that 55°F (13°C) make the fuel generators hard to use. On the plus side the CO_2 enrichment machines using fuel such as natural gas can be hooked directly into a home gas line. No tanks need to be filled, no suspicions aroused.

The fuel generators using natural gas are clean-burning.

Carbon dioxide has several industrial uses such as adding bubbles to soda or charging some fire extinguishers. The bigger the tank, the less often it has to be filled. A grow unit on the pound a month plan (400 watt H.I.D. used for both vegetative growth and flowering, 1000 watt H.I.D. for flowering, 240 watt fluorescent starter) might use a 50 pound tank over 25 days, if CO_2 levels are kept at 1500 ppm. Getting CO_2 can be a hassle because 50 pounds of CO_2 comes in a tank that also weighs about 100 pounds. Smaller tanks are available and are usually used in the soda pop trade. These tanks hold 20 lbs of CO_2. They are much easier to handle. Smaller tanks tend to be more expensive to use because the tanks have to be of high quality to hold pressurized gas. Two small tanks are much more expensive than the one that will hold 50 pounds. The tanks can be rented or bought.

Carbon dioxide enrichment systems using pure gas have six basic parts: 1.) The tank containing CO_2. In this form, CO_2 is pretty harmless although it does replace oxygen in the air. The tank also contains pressurized gas and should be treated with caution. The gas comes out of the tank at very cold temperature, especially at high pressure. Avoid getting the gas on your skin or in your eyes.

2.) A pressure regulator that keeps the pressure of the CO_2 gas constant as it is released from the tank. The pressure regulator is set at 30 pounds per square inch or less. Higher pressure sometimes lead to freezing of the CO_2 line.

3.) A solenoid unit, which is a valve that opens and closes by electrical stimulation releasing the CO_2.

4.) A flow meter which can be set to release a specified amount of CO_2 over an hour's time.

5.) A timer which is used to open and close the solenoid unit at specified times. Inexpensive timers can be used for CO_2 control but highly programmable timers actually save money over a short amount of time. Repeat timers that come on for a short cycle at regular intervals are favored.

Optional, but useful, are sequential timers that control both ventilation and CO_2 disbursement. These timers immobilize the fan that vents air to the outside for a set time during and after the CO_2 is pumped into the growing area. (Several units are available)

6.) Plastic tubing with small holes at set intervals that is used to disperse the CO_2 in the growing area. Since CO_2 is heavier than air the tubing is often installed above the plants. The CO_2 can also be dispersed at one location and blown onto the marijuana with a fan.

On the high priced end are Infrared CO_2 Controllers. These measure CO_2 in the growing area and regulate CO_2 releases to keep levels high. They have gained in popularity as they have come down in price. Because of digital technology, controllers that cost $5,000.00 a few years ago sell now for less than $1,000.00. These controllers take a lot of the guesswork out of CO_2 enrichment. They contain solenoid and flow meters.

If you are not going to shell out for the infrared controller, you will have to use single CO_2 tests ($10) at various times during the growing cycle to monitor the growing units' use of CO_2. Most growers try to keep CO_2 levels at about 3 times the ambient level of 340 ppm or about 1000 ppm. Levels up to 1500 ppm have been used with success.

To figure how much gas you will need, the first thing to determine is the number of cubic feet in the growing area. If there is an area adjacent to the growing space where air is vented and recirculated, this area should be added to the calculation. To figure out the cubic feet multiply the length x width x height of the growing area.

If the growing area is 6 feet wide, 15 feet long, and 8 feet high, you have 720 cubic feet of growing area. This assumes that, except for any venting, this growing area is tightly sealed. A space 4 feet wide by 10 feet long and 6 feet high has 240 cubic feet.

To figure out how much CO_2 is needed to enrich a growing area the cubic feet of the growing area are multiplied by set numbers. These numbers are arrived at by determining the level of CO_2 enrichment desired and assume an ambient CO_2 level of 300 ppm.

The numbers follow:

1000	parts per million	.0007
1100	ppm	.0008
1200	ppm	.0009
1300	ppm	.0010
1400	ppm	.0011
1500	ppm	.0012

To figure how much CO_2 is needed multiply a number from this series by the cubic feet in the growing area. If you have 720 cubic feet as in the example above and want to bring CO_2 levels to 1500 ppm, multiply 720 x .0012. You need .86 cubic feet of gas to bring the CO_2 level to 1500 ppm. (Note: One pound of pure CO_2 under pressure equals 8.7 cubic feet of CO_2 at room temperature.) To bring 240 cubic feet of growing space as in the second example above to 1000 ppm, multiply 240 x.0007. You need .17 cubic feet of CO_2 to achieve this.

This figure tells you how much CO_2 you need, but not how often you will have to enrich. If you look at every marijuana leaf as a light and CO_2 collector, it becomes clear that the bigger the plants the more often enrichment is needed. Up to 3 hours between enrichment cycles can be used when plants are small. Cycles of 1 hour or less are usually used on plants that fill the growing area, but a number of factors have to be considered. Is a space adjacent to the growing also being enriched? Will the needed amount of gas be best delivered in one shot or shorter bursts?

Take the example above with 720 cubic feet of grow space. We will assume the grower has a repeat timer to control the enrichment cycles. You need .86 cubic feet of CO_2 to bring this space up to 1500 ppm (maximum enrichment). Round off the .86 to 1 cubic foot because it will make life easier. When the plants are small they will devour the CO_2 over about 3 hours. The grower decides to deliver 1/3 of the CO_2, .33 cubic feet each hour, so the enrichment cycle will be programmed to last 15 minutes, .25 hours. To figure out the flow rate needed for this divide .33 by .25. In this case the flow meter is set to release 1.3 cubic feet per hour.

When this 720 cubic foot space is teaming with large, vigorous marijuana plants you can almost hear the plants drawing in available CO_2. More CO_2 is needed. About 1 cubic foot of CO_2 per hour is needed to keep levels at the maximum, (1500 ppm). Use a CO_2 tester to determine more precisely how much CO_2 the plants are using. If the same 15 minute (.25 hours) cycle as above is used to deliver the CO_2, you need a flow rate of 4 cubic feet per hour (1 divided by .25).

The same grower may have shelled out for an expensive timer, and so wants to deliver the 1 cubic foot of CO_2 in two 10 minute cycles each hour. The grower wants to deliver .5 cubic feet of CO_2 in .166 hours (10 minutes divided by 60 minutes. A flow rate of about 3 cubic feet of CO_2 per hour is needed (.5 divided by .166).

The other factor that needs to be taken into consideration is the venting of the growing area to the outside. Where the air goes, so goes the CO_2. You want to vent as far from the enrichment cycle as possible. Controllers containing tandem timers are made specifically for this. A good timer can also be used. The space can be vented for ten minutes before the enrichment cycle, and then not again for as long as possible. Temperature will be the deciding factor. The space needs venting when the temperature reaches 85°F. The closed system (next section) uses an air conditioner to keep temperature and humidity down, so little or no ventilation to the outside is needed.

Growers using CO_2 generators that burn hydrocarbons use the same calculations for the amount of CO_2 needed for enrichment. These machines are rated by how many cubic feet of CO_2 per hour they deliver. If the machine produces 4 cubic feet of CO_2 per hour, for example, and the space requires 1 cubic foot per hour for enrichment, the machine is run for 15 minutes each hour. A gallon of fuel weighs about 4 pounds and produces 10-12 pounds of CO_2.

The Closed System

The closed system operates by enriching the air around plants with CO_2, and seldom venting air to the outside. One of the biggest problem indoor growers have, especially in crowded urban areas, is the pungent scent of marijuana escaping from the grow room and wafting over the neighborhood, leading to potential detection. Usually this occurs because fans are used to remove excess heat. With a closed system this is avoided.

No-work closed systems are easy to set up in cooler growing spaces. If the temperatures outside are colder than 55°F the space will need little ventilation to the outside. Basement spaces are often cooler than other areas of a building. Frequently the heat from the lights is enough to heat the growing area. If the actual growing area makes up 20% or less of the area defined as the grow room, marijuana growers can get by simply by recirculating the air. If water is used judiciously and the growing area has good interior air movement, problems with high humidity can be minimized.

Add CO_2 and there is no reason to vent air to the outside. The only reason to vent to the outside is to dissipate humidity, which can cause mold late in the flowering cycle. Many growers run their lights at night when temperatures are cooler so as to be able to run a closed system. Closed systems are harder to set up if there are many lights packed into a small area, especially if there is no adjacent space where air from the growing area can be cooled and recirculated.

When temperatures are higher than 55°F closed systems can still be relatively easy and cost effective to set up. An air conditioning unit run on "recirculate" is added to cool the air. As air conditioners cool the air they also remove water from it. Control of humidity is the key to establishing a closed system. A vent has to be added to the unit but it removes only waste heat and humidity. Little odor will escape. Air conditioning units for use in the center of a room have also become available. They look like portable heaters but have a small vent line for water and heat. Since marijuana, under CO_2 enrichment, will grow prolifically in temperatures as high as 85°F, in most cases the air conditioning unit will not have to operate excessively.

System to System Enrichment

We have seen that plants are CO_2 gatherers. There is another element of this growth process of interest to the marijuana cultivator. It is called respiration. Respiration is an integral plant process used to oxidize and use the CO_2 plants take in. A growth equation for a plant could be stated as CO_2

taken in, less respiration, equals growth. A lot of CO_2 is released during respiration. Growers can farm and use this CO_2 .

Unlike CO_2, which is taken in only in light, respiration occurs all the time, but at a faster rate in warmer temperatures. In darkness marijuana actually releases sizable amounts of CO_2. In an indoor marijuana growing area in bloom (12 hours of darkness) CO_2 levels can build up to twice the ambient 350ppm level after a few hours of darkness.

Growers with multiple light systems can take advantage of the fact that plants emit CO_2 in darkness. As an example, take a grower who has two high intensity lights, one 400 watt and one 1000 watt light, plus a few fluorescent lights for starting plants. The 1000 watt light is probably in the flowering area, which is on for 12 hours, and the 400 watt in the vegetative growth area, on 18 - 24 hours. If the grower has a CO_2 system but wants to conserve gas he or she can farm the CO_2 from the flowering system when it is dark and use it on plants on the longer light cycles of vegetative growth. A small fan is used to move the CO_2 from one system to the other. The potential downside to this system is that by connecting the systems, problems like insect infestations are quickly spread to all plants.

Postscript

You can increase the effective yield from your garden by using the leaf from your marijuana plants. Although marijuana leaf makes a harsh smoke, it contains sizable amounts of cannabinoids. Often 10% or more of a crops' THC is in the leaves. The leaves are quite effective for use in cooking and can be concentrated by making extracts or tinctures. The Marijuana Herbal Cookbook by Tom Flowers contains the latest information on cooking and making medicines from the Cannabis plant.

index